© 2018 agoodmovietowatch, all rights reserved. This book may not be reproduced in whole or in part, stored in a retrieval system, or transmitted in any form or by any means - electronic, mechanical, or other - without written permission from the publisher, except by a reviewer, who may quote brief passages in a review. For more information, contact the publisher at agoodmovietowatch.com/contact

Many of the reviews featured in this book have been submitted to us by our users. We would like to take the opportunity to say thank you for the continued trust and support.
A full list of contributors can be found at the end of the book.

Netflix is a trademarked brands, all rights reserved. Netflix guide is not produced or endorsed by Netflix, nor do the creators of this book or of agoodmovietowatch.com have any affiliation with Netflix or any other VOD providers. All images, names, and trademarks are also copyright and the property of their respective owners, they are featured in this book as criticism falling under 'fair use' as provided for in section 107 of the US Copyright Law. Furthermore, availability of titles is fully controlled by Netflix, and the makers of this book have no control over the selection of movies and TV shows that Netflix chooses to add or remove, therefore the movies and shows marked as available are not always guaranteed to be so.

This guide only has movies and shows that were loved by critics and viewers: titles that have a high score on IMDb combined with a high score on Rotten Tomatoes.

Introduction: note from the founder

It was on an exchange semester in Seoul, Korea, when I realized that there wasn't a platform dedicated to the task of helping me figure out what to watch. By chance, I landed on Short Term 12 (starring Brie Larson) and was blown away by the acting, aesthetic, and narrative. I later found out that the film was (undeservingly) a commercial failure. I decided to start agoodmovietowatch.com as both the platform I wanted to sift through the mainstream recommendations and to serve as a link between movies like Short Term 12 and their deserved audiences.

Initially, the idea was to have a simple one-button website that would give the user a random good movie available to watch instantly on streaming services. I realized quickly that things were going to be more challenging; so I started exploring new ways to suggest movies to the growing number of users. I developed new navigation paths (mood, With, MoviesLike, etc); and kept evolving the website's design and concept to respond to the need for a similar platform, as well as the ever-changing experience of movie viewing.

Today, I am very happy to present the next step in that process: A guide-book to the world of On-Demand.

I want this book to be something you leave by your tea table, something you write on, something you wear out, and don't mind if your kids scribble on it. In a way, I want it to be the magazine in the dentist's office that looks as old as the dentist. I want this book to be everywhere, and to be timeless, to bring light to the unfairly little-known movies that it recommends, while solving the frustration of not knowing what to watch.

The obvious challenge with choosing this medium for this project is that the Netflix catalogue is not stable. Almost every week, titles leave and others are added. To fix this, the movies are divided into three categories: The Very Best, The Originals (which will never expire), and The Suggestions. Our aim is to also come out with a new edition every three months, keeping you updated with the freshest – good- movies and shows on Netflix.

Bilal Zou

Glossary by mood

A-list actors	10, 24, 28, 29, 35, 41, 74, 85
Absorbing	2, 3, 24, 34, 38, 39, 48, 50, 58, 63, 64, 82, 86, 87
Action-packed	1, 3, 5, 76
Beautiful	8, 17, 19, 20, 21, 27, 31, 35, 39, 42, 45, 52, 56, 59, 60, 65, 87, 90, 93
Challenging	1, 25, 38, 47, 57, 58, 68, 79, 82, 83, 95
Character-driven	21, 23, 25, 27, 30, 38, 42, 43, 81
Charming	4, 8, 10, 11, 13, 17, 19, 21, 22, 39, 88, 91, 93
Cool	22, 44
Cute	10, 12, 19, 39
Dark	18, 49, 54, 81, 83
Depressing	15, 20, 27, 29, 57, 66, 69
Dramatic	1, 23, 36, 37, 39, 41, 42, 77
Easy	7, 19, 22
Emotional	20, 24, 25, 36, 37, 39, 41, 54, 55, 71
Funny	6, 8, 9, 13, 17, 50, 75, 81
Goofy	12, 14, 15
Gripping	25, 33, 39, 49, 52, 58, 71, 73, 77, 95, 96
Grown-up Comedy	7, 8, 15, 16, 17, 18, 19, 21, 36
Grown-up Romance	21, 35, 87
Happy	10, 17, 22
Heart-warming	12, 19, 24, 31, 36, 39
Humane	7, 17, 20, 23, 24, 25, 26, 34, 37, 38, 39, 43, 48, 52, 57, 60, 61, 62, 70, 72, 90, 91
Inspiring	3, 54, 57, 59, 61, 62, 63, 64, 67, 70
Instructive	46, 48, 51, 53, 54, 56, 63, 65, 67, 69, 70, 72
Intense	1, 26, 32, 45, 46, 58, 68, 74, 76, 78, 86
Lighthearted	10, 14, 19
Long	44, 66
Lovely	10, 11, 19, 24, 36, 39
Mysterious	77, 78, 83, 95
No-brainer	10, 12, 14, 84, 88
Original	50, 81, 83, 86, 90
Powerful	20
Raw	1, 3, 12, 26, 33, 41, 48, 73, 74, 81, 96

Relatable	17, 23
Romantic	86, 88, 89, 93
Simple	8, 10, 12, 14, 15, 17, 19, 36, 88, 93
Sincere	20, 39
Slow	15, 28
Smart	25, 50, 54
Sunday	4, 8, 19, 21, 25, 35, 44, 46, 52, 54, 61, 70, 71
Suspenseful	49, 77, 78
Sweet	12, 21, 22, 93
Thought-provoking	4, 18, 20, 23, 25, 26, 28, 33, 39, 45, 46, 47, 48, 49, 51, 52, 54, 55, 57, 58, 62, 63, 65, 66, 72, 77, 86, 91, 94, 95
Thrilling	1, 2, 25, 49, 64, 76, 79, 85
Touching	7, 20, 23, 24, 26, 34
True-crime	15, 49, 58, 68
true-story-based	1, 3, 15, 23, 24, 40, 58, 60, 64
Uplifting	8, 14, 22, 24, 64, 93
Violent	80, 81
Warm	10, 11, 12, 19, 21, 22, 23, 24, 31, 36, 39, 87, 88
Weird	15, 18, 74, 75, 77, 81, 90, 95
Well-acted	3, 8, 18, 20, 21, 24, 25, 26, 37, 40, 43, 82, 85, 91, 92

Action

ACTION | **THE VERY BEST** | 1

City of God 2002

★★★★★

This movie will punch, kick and slap the crap out of you. Something that will be hard to believe after you watch it – it is based on a true story. Filmed and set in the poverty-stricken favelas of Rio de Janeiro, it follows two young men who choose two opposite paths; one an aspiring drug leader and the other an aspiring photographer. City of God is their story; a movie filled with great performances (from mostly non-professionals), and an experience that is as compelling as it is adrenaline-inducing.

WATCH IT IF IN THE MOOD FOR SOMETHING:
Action-packed, Challenging, Dramatic, Intense, Raw, Thrilling, true-story-based

RATING:
R

LANGUAGE:
Spanish

STARRING:
Alexandre Rodrigues, Leandro Firmino, Matheus Nachtergaele

WRITTEN BY:
Bráulio Mantovani, Paulo Lins

DIRECTED BY:
Fernando Meirelles, Kátia Lund

ACTION | **THE VERY BEST** | 2

Battle Royale 2000

★★★★★

When asked about this film, Quentin Tarantino goes so far as to say, "If there's any movie that's been made since I've been making movies that I wish I had made, it's that one." Kinji Fukasaku's cult classic follows an alternative reality set in Japan, where a random high school class is forced onto a remote island to fight to the death. While it does follow the quintessential 'only one shall leave' scenario (complete with over-the-top, almost comedic murder scenes), the raw emotion and character depth cuts far deeper than traditional action thrillers. The film will leave you out of breath but still satisfied with how the narrative plays out.

WATCH IT IF IN THE MOOD FOR SOMETHING:
Absorbing, Thrilling

RATING:
Not Rated

LANGUAGE:
English

STARRING:
Aki Maeda, Tarô Yamamoto, Tatsuya Fujiwara

WRITTEN BY:
Kenta Fukasaku

DIRECTED BY:
Kinji Fukasaku

ACTION | **THE ORIGINALS** | 3

The Siege of Jadotville

2016

★★★★☆

The Siege of Jadotville is a different kind of war movie. It doesn't recount famous battles or portray renowned heroes – instead, it's about heroes and events that went completely unnoticed. Namely, the Irish 35 Battalion 'A' Company – a group of youngsters who are sent out on a U.N mission to the Congo. What was supposed to be a simple positioning quickly becomes one of the most sought-after locations and the battalion of 150 'war-virgins" find themselves up against 3000 mercenaries led by experienced French commandants. And what a tribute this film is: it's well-paced, powerfully shot, and the acting, led by Jamie Dornan on one side and Guillaume Canet on the other, is absolutely perfect.

WATCH IT IF IN THE MOOD FOR SOMETHING:
Absorbing, Action-packed, Inspiring, Raw, true-story-based, Well-acted

RATING:
Not Rated

LANGUAGE:
English

STARRING:
Jamie Dornan, Jason O'Mara, Mark Strong

WRITTEN BY:
Kevin Brodbin

DIRECTED BY:
Richie Smyth

ACTION | **THE ORIGINALS** | 4

Okja 2017

★★★★★

Director Bong Joon-ho (Snowpiercer) does something quite amazing with the $50 million budget Netflix gave him: he makes a simplistic movie. But man, is it good. Okja tells the story of a "super pig" experiment that sends genetically modified pigs to top farmers around the world. In Korea, a farmer's granddaughter forms a special relationship with one of these super pigs (Okja). When the company who originally ran the experiment want their pig back (performances by Jake Gyllenhaal and Tilda Swinton) – the two find an ally in an animal advocacy group led by Jay (Paul Dano). This is a straightforward movie, but nevertheless it is entertaining and full of thought-provoking themes and performances from an excellent cast.

WATCH IT IF IN THE MOOD FOR SOMETHING:
Charming, Sunday, Thought-provoking

RATING:
TV-MA

LANGUAGE:
English, Korean

STARRING:
Jake Gyllenhaal, Paul Dano, Seo-Hyun Ahn, Tilda Swinton

WRITTEN BY:
Jon Ronson, Joon-ho Bong

DIRECTED BY:
Joon-ho Bong

ACTION | **THE SUGGESTIONS** | 5

Ip Man 2008

★★★★★

It's been acclaimed as one the best Kung Fu movies ever made. You are probably wondering why this contemporary movie made that short list when its genre had its peak decades ago: it is visually striking and at the same time surprisingly story-oriented. As you would expect of course, there is quite a fair amount of action scenes, but the characters are also brilliant which is very uncommon in this type of movie. It is an exciting movie, and worthy of any compliment or good rating it may get.

WATCH IT IF IN THE MOOD FOR SOMETHING:
Action-packed

RATING:
R

LANGUAGE:
Cantonese

STARRING:
Donnie Yen, Simon Yam, Siu-Wong Fan

WRITTEN BY:
Edmond Wong, Tai-lee Chan

DIRECTED BY:
Wilson Yip

ACTION | **THE SUGGESTIONS** | 6

Trollhunter 2010

★★★★☆

Filmed as a "found footage" of a Norwegian college film crew investigating local poachers, this movie really surprised me. To be fair, I didn't really know what to expect. But I definitely didn't expect to like this movie as much as I did. The pacing is on point. The suspense hits you at just the right times. There are a few drops of humour trickled throughout to keep a smile on your face. And that's how my face stayed when the credits rolled.

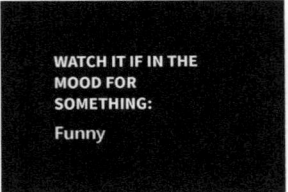

WATCH IT IF IN THE MOOD FOR SOMETHING:
Funny

RATING:
PG-13

LANGUAGE:
Norwegian

STARRING:
Anton Yelchin,
Kelsey Grammer,
Lexi Medrano

WRITTEN BY:
Guillermo del Toro

DIRECTED BY:
André Øvredal

Comedy

COMEDY | **THE VERY BEST** | 7

St. Vincent 2014

★★★★★

In this comedy/drama, Bill Murray plays an aged, dispirited war veteran named Vincent who openly disdains most people and gives little attention to anything beyond alcohol and horse racing. Living a life of solitude in Brooklyn, everything takes a turn when a young single mother (Melissa McCarthy) and her son Oliver move in next door. Vincent eventually takes on the responsibility of watching over Oliver when Maggie is at work. Murray is perfectly unpleasant in his darkly comedic role, as his relationship with Oliver evolves despite his own misgivings, providing young Oliver (Jaeden Lieberher) with the fatherly/grandfatherly presence he desperately needs. Though somewhat formulaic, St. Vincent rises above expectations by way of great dialogue, favourable performances from all of the leads, and an unbelievably touching finale that will melt your heart. Much better than you probably expect— definitely check this one out.

WATCH IT IF IN THE MOOD FOR SOMETHING:
Easy, Grown-up Comedy, Humane, Touching

 RATING:
PG-13

 LANGUAGE:
English

 STARRING:
Bill Murray, Melissa McCarthy, Naomi Watts

 WRITTEN BY:
Theodore Melfi

 DIRECTED BY:
Theodore Melfi

COMEDY | **THE ORIGINALS** | 8

The Fundamentals of Caring 2016

★★★★☆

The Fundamentals of Caring is an offbeat comedy/drama starring Paul Rudd as Ben, a man attempting to overcome tragedy and looming divorce by becoming the caretaker for a teenager with muscular dystrophy (Craig Roberts, Submarine). The two develop an unconventional relationship based largely on sarcasm and profanity, delivering many laugh-out-loud moments, while also slowly exposing the pain each is carrying inside. Together, at Ben's urging, they embark on a road trip across the western United States for Craig to see the world beyond his wheelchair and television. It's a formulaic yet fun and touching road movie that covers much familiar ground, but also offers a fine illustration of caregiving, personal growth, and emotional healing. Paul Rudd is as good ever, and Roberts is utterly superb. One of the best movies on the Netflix Originals catalogue, and an undeniable winner, all-in-all.

WATCH IT IF IN THE MOOD FOR SOMETHING:
Beautiful, Charming, Funny, Grown-up Comedy, Simple, Sunday, Uplifting, Well-acted

RATING:
Not Rated

LANGUAGE:
English

STARRING:
Craig Roberts, Paul Rudd, Selena Gomez

WRITTEN BY:
Jonathan Evison, Rob Burnett

DIRECTED BY:
Rob Burnett, Robert Meyer Burnett

COMEDY | **THE SUGGESTIONS** | 9

Hot Fuzz 2007

★★★★★

One of the many good movies from director Edgar Wright – if you loved Shaun of the Dead, then this Buddy-Cop Homage will make you double over (and question humanity – or lack, thereof) just as much. Sandford is a small English village with the lowest crime and murder rates, so when overachieving police Nicholas Angel (Simon Pegg) gets sent there because he was so good he intimidated those around him, he just about loses it. From car-chasing, bone-thrilling, head-blowing action, he graduates to swan-calling, thrill-seeking, sleep-inducing madness. But all that's about to change – for the worse? For the better? You decide.

An obscenely funny flick that has an intriguing plot and an even greater set of characters, Hot Fuzz wasn't named the best film of the Cornetto trilogy for nothing, clearly cementing Pegg and Nick Frost as the ultimate action duo of the genre.

WATCH IT IF IN THE MOOD FOR SOMETHING:
Funny

RATING:
R

LANGUAGE:
English

STARRING:
Martin Freeman, Nick Frost, Simon Pegg

WRITTEN BY:
Edgar Wright, Simon Pegg

DIRECTED BY:
Edgar Wright

COMEDY | **THE SUGGESTIONS** | 10

Begin Again 2013

★★★★☆

John Carney, who directed the critically and commercially successful Once, may be the world's best captor of charm. Begin Again tells the story of a broken-hearted singer who gets discovered by a failed showbiz executive. Their ideas and love for music are all they have to face their failures and bring their creativity to life. The original songs are charming and from Keira Knightley and Mark Ruffalo to Yasiin Bey (Mos Def), Adam Levine, and Cee-Lo Green, the cast generate sparkling chemistry and portray the story beautifully. Begin again is a sweet and effortless watch, yet far from being your classic rom-com.

WATCH IT IF IN THE MOOD FOR SOMETHING:
A-list actors, Charming, Cute, Happy, Lighthearted, Lovely, No-brainer, Simple, Warm

RATING:
R

LANGUAGE:
English

STARRING:
Adam Levine, Keira Knightley, Mark Ruffalo

WRITTEN BY:
John Carney

DIRECTED BY:
John Carney

COMEDY | **THE SUGGESTIONS** | 11

Moonrise Kingdom 2012

★★★★★

Two twelve year olds: Sam, an introverted Khaki scout (Jared Gilman) and the sharp yet sassy Suzy (Kara Hayward), fall in love and run away to their own personal paradise they call "Moonrise Kingdom." The young girl's parents (Bill Murray and Frances McDormand) call the authorities. A search party compiled of the local Sheriff (Bruce Willis), Khaki Scout Troop Leader (Edward Norton) and his scouts along with an assortment of other characters try to track down the young runaways through the wilderness.

The characters are as bright, quirky and colourful as their surroundings. The film's trademark stylistic handmade art direction (Wes Anderson) and clever camera choices add character to the storytelling. Even with its sweet and playful demeanour, major real world issues such as bullying and infidelity are touched upon. Moonrise Kingdom is a delightfully charming film with a meticulously executed plot and sophisticated humour.

WATCH IT IF IN THE MOOD FOR SOMETHING:
Charming, Lovely, Warm

RATING:
MPAA PG-13

LANGUAGE:
English

STARRING:
Bruce Willis, Jared Gilman, Kara Hayward

WRITTEN BY:
Roman Coppola, Wes Anderson

DIRECTED BY:
Wes Anderson

COMEDY | **THE SUGGESTIONS** | 12

Goon 2012

★★★★☆

Goon is funny, violent, and sweet as hell. You'll be surprised by how nasty it is but at the same time you won't care. What you will want to do, on the other hand, is rip through the screen, and hug the main character. It is also a great example of a feel-good movie that isn't solely focused on being a feel-good movie. It's also great love story, with all its absurdities and highly emotional load. The story shines a light on the players who join hockey teams not for the game but for the fights that may erupt. They are called goons. Doug Glatt (Seann William Scott) is a new goon and this movie is his journey towards success both on the ice and off.

WATCH IT IF IN THE MOOD FOR SOMETHING:
Cute, Goofy, Heartwarming, No-brainer, Raw, Simple, Sweet

 RATING:
 R

 LANGUAGE:
English

 STARRING:
Alison Pill, Jay Baruchel, Seann William Scott

WRITTEN BY:
Evan Goldberg, Jay Baruchel

 **DIRECTED BY:**
Michael Dowse

COMEDY | **THE SUGGESTIONS** | 13

The Wackness 2008

★★★★☆

A period comedy set in New York in the summer of 1994, the Wackness is a coming of age story about Luke Shapiro (Joshua Peck), as he deals with family trauma, love, and economic hardship while selling pot to his strange psychologist. Rescued from a somewhat typical bildungsroman plot by sharp character acting, a firm directorial hand and an absolutely fitting soundtrack that evokes the golden age of rap music.

WATCH IT IF IN THE MOOD FOR SOMETHING:
Charming, Funny, whimsical

RATING:
R

LANGUAGE:
English

STARRING:
Ben Kingsley, Josh Peck, Olivia Thirlby

WRITTEN BY:
Jonathan Levine

DIRECTED BY:
Jonathan Levine

COMEDY | **THE SUGGESTIONS** | 14

I Love You, Man 2009

★★★★☆

"Sweet sweet hangin". I Love You, Man hits a cosiness more movies should aspire to be. It has smart jokes sprinkled throughout the very visible chemistry between Rudd and Segel. Their courtship is hysterical and relatable. I Love You, Man sets a high standard for bromances: they must be fantastic! It is a simple yet a brilliant feel-good movie.

WATCH IT IF IN THE MOOD FOR SOMETHING:
Goofy, Lighthearted, No-brainer, Simple, Uplifting

RATING:
MPAA R

LANGUAGE:
English

STARRING:
Jason Segel, Paul Rudd, Rashida Jones

WRITTEN BY:
John Hamburg, Larry Levin

DIRECTED BY:
John Hamburg

COMEDY | **THE SUGGESTIONS** | 15

Bernie 2012

★★★☆☆

This is not what you are looking for if you are not into slow movies. It ambles along like the East-Texas drawls that populate it, taking its sweet time and letting the story gradually roll out. This true-story-based film is driven by a strong and witty performance from Jack Black –just not the Jack Black you know. A different kind of movie, Bernie is an entertaining mix of true crime and comedy.

WATCH IT IF IN THE MOOD FOR SOMETHING:
Depressing, Goofy, Grown-up Comedy, Simple, Slow, True-crime, true-story-based, Weird

RATING:
PG-13

LANGUAGE:
English

STARRING:
Jack Black, Matthew McConaughey, Shirley MacLaine

WRITTEN BY:
Richard Linklater

DIRECTED BY:
Richard Linklater

COMEDY | **THE SUGGESTIONS** | 16

The Meyerowitz Stories

2017

★★★★☆

From director Noah Baumbach (Frances Ha, The Squid and the Whale) The Meyerowitz Stories is a beautiful family comedy otherwise known as that Adam Sandler that doesn't suck. He plays a recently divorced man, as he usually does, called Danny (as he's usually called). Danny moves in with his father, played by Dustin Hoffman, who himself is dealing with feelings of failure. As both of them are joined by other members of the family (including Danny's half-brother, played by Ben Stiller), their family dynamic comes to the surface in a beautiful, sometimes very moving way. This is an amazingly tender movie in which Noah Baumbach proves he's so good, he can make even Adam Sandler sound genuine.

WATCH IT IF IN THE MOOD FOR SOMETHING:
Grown-up Comedy

RATING:
TV-MA

LANGUAGE:
English

STARRING:
Adam Sandler, Ben Stiller, Dustin Hoffman, Grace Van Patten

WRITTEN BY:
Noah Baumbach

DIRECTED BY:
Noah Baumbach

COMEDY | **THE SUGGESTIONS** | 17

Frances Ha 2013

★★★☆☆

Frances (Greta Gerwig) lives in New York – but not the glamorous NYC of Woody Allen movies. Taking place primarily in the gritty and rapidly gentrifying North Brooklyn, the black and white film paints a picture of an extended adolescence. Focusing on the goofy and carefree Frances, who loses her boyfriend, her best friend and her dream of being a dancer. She moves in with two guys, both of whom are more successful than her, and becomes even more determined to fulfil her goals, impractical as they may be. Fans of HBO's Girls and other odes to not being a "real person" yet will love this film.

WATCH IT IF IN THE MOOD FOR SOMETHING:
Beautiful, Charming, Funny, Grown-up Comedy, Happy, Humane, Relatable, Satisfying, Simple

 RATING:
R

 LANGUAGE:
English

 STARRING:
Adam Driver, Greta Gerwig, Mickey Sumner

 WRITTEN BY:
Greta Gerwig, Noah Baumbach

DIRECTED BY:
Noah Baumbach

COMEDY | **THE SUGGESTIONS** | 18

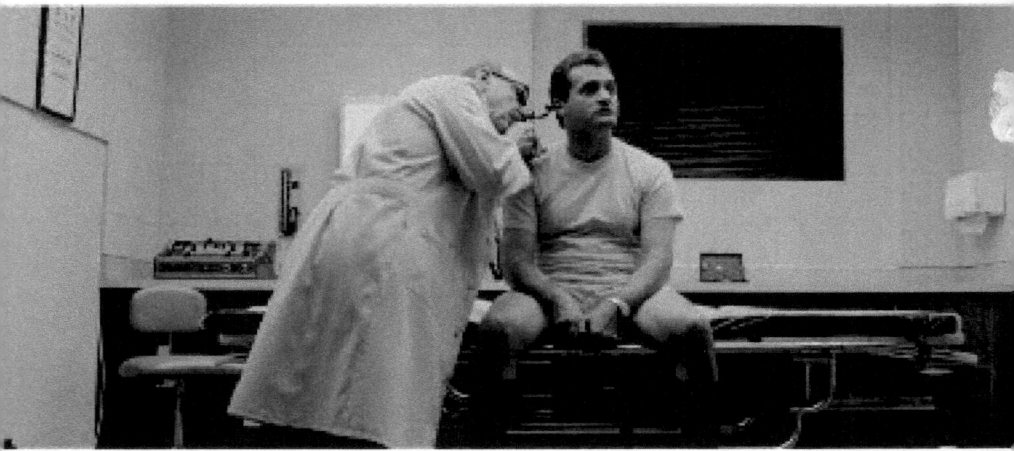

A Serious Man 2009

★★★☆☆

A Serious Man is an almost inexplicable and philosophically dark comedy from the Cohen Brothers. Its protagonist, Larry, is a professor at a quiet university whose wife decides to leave him for one of his more successful colleagues. His unemployed brother moves on to the couch and both of his kids start acting out. He starts a quest for meaning and clarity within his Jewish community. The movie's aesthetics and comedy will be appreciated by all Cohen Brothers fans. However, the intricacies and struggle of the protagonist will hit home for anyone who has had a religious upbringing: Jewish guilt, and by extension Catholic guilt (or any other religious guilt) are big themes here. An original, weird, hard to understand masterpiece. Other than the prologue, you'll feel like you have to watch it many times to understand it. The film earned itself many nominations for the Oscars, including Best Picture.

WATCH IT IF IN THE MOOD FOR SOMETHING:
Dark, Grown-up Comedy, Thought-provoking, Weird, Well-acted

 RATING:
 R

 LANGUAGE:
English

STARRING:
Michael Stuhlbarg, Richard Kind, Sari Lennick

 WRITTEN BY:
Ethan Coen, Joel Coen

 DIRECTED BY:
Ethan Coen, Joel Coen

COMEDY | **THE SUGGESTIONS** | 19

People Places Things

2015

★★★★☆

«When comedians get a bit older they do a movie with "emotions" in it. Here's mine.» Flight of the Conchords' Jemaine Clement on Twitter. People Places Things is exactly that, a funny yet heartfelt comedy. Will Henry, A New York City graphic novelist walks in on his girlfriend cheating on him at their kids' birthday party. A year later, Will is struggling to define his new life as a single parent while still getting over his breakup. Smart, honest, and led by Jemaine Clement, this film will strike you in its simplicity but will hold you with its charm.

WATCH IT IF IN THE MOOD FOR SOMETHING:
Beautiful, Charming, Cute, Easy, Grown-up Comedy, Heartwarming, Lighthearted, Lovely, Simple, Sunday

 RATING:
R

 LANGUAGE:
English

 STARRING:
Jemaine Clement, Jessica Williams, Regina Hall

 WRITTEN BY:
Jim Strouse

 DIRECTED BY:
Jim Strouse

Drama

DRAMA | **THE VERY BEST** | 20

Mustang 2015

★★★★★

Five orphaned sister are put under house arrest by their uncle and grandmother after they are seen horsing around with local boys from school. While their actions were purely innocent, their behaviour is viewed as scandalous and shameful by the conservative elders in their small Turkish village. After this incident, their grandmother turns her attention towards marrying off her granddaughters. Each of the five sisters rebel in their own way, but it is the youngest and rowdiest sister, Lale, who is the central protagonist of the film. She watches helplessly as each of her older sisters are married off with an increasing sense of dread and desperation. While this may sound hopelessly depressing, the movie is equal parts beautiful and tragic, and floats across the screen in a dreamlike manner. Not all of the sisters escape their oppressive surroundings or their assigned fate, but the message is clear: it's crucial to try.

WATCH IT IF IN THE MOOD FOR SOMETHING:
Beautiful, Depressing, Emotional, Humane, Important, Insightful, Powerful, Sincere, Thought-provoking, Touching, Well-acted

RATING:
PG-13

LANGUAGE:
Turkish

STARRING:
Doga Zeynep Doguslu, Günes Sensoy, Tugba Sunguroglu

WRITTEN BY:
Alice Winocour, Deniz Gamze Ergüven

DIRECTED BY:
Deniz Gamze Ergüven

DRAMA | **THE VERY BEST** | 21

Blue Jay 2016

★★★★★

Shot in black and white to be the best dialogue-driven, character-study film it can be; Blue Jay stars Sarah Paulson and Mark Duplass in a cozy, slow-burning film. Their characters, respectively Amanda and Jim, are former high-school sweethearts who run into each other in their hometown 20 years later. They talk, they get coffee, and then beer and jelly beans, until they find themselves to Jim's mother's house. As they familiarize themselves again, and the movie moves forward, it abandons its romantic chops to become a truly heartfelt and real film. A revelation of a movie.

WATCH IT IF IN THE MOOD FOR SOMETHING:
Beautiful, Character-driven, Charming, Grown-up Comedy, Grown-up Romance, Sunday, Sweet, Warm, Well-acted

RATING:
Not Rated

LANGUAGE:
English

STARRING:
Clu Gulager, Mark Duplass, Sarah Paulson

WRITTEN BY:
Mark Duplass

DIRECTED BY:
Alexandre Lehmann

DRAMA | **THE VERY BEST** | 22

Sing Street 2016

★★★★★

In 1980s Dublin, a young Irish catholic-school boy, whose family is facing financial problems starts his own band with the sole objective of impressing a mysterious femme fatale. The film takes you on a beautiful and witty journey through the band's path to success and our protagonist's quest in conquering his love all to the rhythm of some of the biggest 80's pop-rock hits and the band's own original soundtrack. Without a doubt this film is the long awaited passion project of filmmaker John Carney (Once, Begin Again).

WATCH IT IF IN THE MOOD FOR SOMETHING:
Charming, Cool, Easy, Happy, Sweet, Uplifting, Warm

RATING:
PG-13

LANGUAGE:
English

STARRING:
Aidan Gillen, Ferdia Walsh-Peelo, Maria Doyle Kennedy

WRITTEN BY:
John Carney

DIRECTED BY:
John Carney

DRAMA | **THE VERY BEST** | 23

Fruitvale Station 2013

★★★★★

The true story of Oscar Grant III, a 22-year-old black man on the last day of 2008, where his will to change is challenged by his past and the police. You've probably read and heard a lot about young black mens' encounters with the police, and for this reason you might feel like skipping this film. Don't. Produced by Academy Award winner Forest Whitaker, it is compassionate and powerfully told, that it surpasses the sadness of its subject matter to be a celebration of life. It is an extraordinary film and important watch.

WATCH IT IF IN THE MOOD FOR SOMETHING:
Character-driven, Dramatic, Humane, Relatable, Thought-provoking, Touching, true-story-based, Warm

RATING:
R

LANGUAGE:
English

STARRING:
Melonie Diaz, Michael B. Jordan, Octavia Spencer

WRITTEN BY:
Ryan Coogler

DIRECTED BY:
Ryan Coogler

DRAMA | THE VERY BEST | 24

Lion 2016

★★★★★

Lion is the award-sweeping movie based on the true story of a kid in India who gets lost in a train and suddenly finds himself thousands of kilometers away from home. 25 years later, after being adopted by an Australian couple, he embarks on a journey through his memory and across continents to reconnect with his lost family. Dev Patel plays Saroo, and Nicole Kidman plays his Australian adoptive mother. Two truly amazing performances that will transport you to the time and place of the events, as well as its emotions spanning tear-jerking moments and pure joy. An uplifting, meaningful, and beautiful movie.

WATCH IT IF IN THE MOOD FOR SOMETHING:
A-list actors, Absorbing, Emotional, Heart-warming, Humane, Lovely, Touching, true-story-based, Uplifting, Well-acted

RATING:
PG-13

LANGUAGE:
Bengali, English, Hindi

STARRING:
Dev Patel, Nicole Kidman, Rooney Mara

WRITTEN BY:
Luke Davies, Saroo Brierley

DIRECTED BY:
Garth Davis

DRAMA | **THE VERY BEST** | 25

Gook 2017

★★★★★

Two Korean-American brothers run their family's shoe store on the day of the 1992 LA riots. The day starts in their struggling business as they hang out with their friend – an 11-year-old African American girl – Kamilla. The Rodney King verdict is announced and violence breaks out. Written, directed, and starring Justin Chon, it's a tight 94 minutes of impressive film-making that speaks volumes about America's intra-minority race relations. It's a work that elicits sympathy, and manages to uplift the violent event to a human level. An amazing movie.

WATCH IT IF IN THE MOOD FOR SOMETHING:
Challenging, Character-driven, Emotional, Gripping, Humane, Smart, Sunday, Thought-provoking, Thrilling, Well-acted

RATING:
Unrated

LANGUAGE:
English

STARRING:
Curtiss Cook Jr., Justin Chon, Simone Baker

WRITTEN BY:
Justin Chon

DIRECTED BY:
Justin Chon

Beasts of No Nation 2015

★★★★★

An instant classic, Beast of No Nation is a unique and uniquely-paced war drama which ranges in patterns from explosive visual storytelling to calm character studies. A child joins a rebel group consisting almost entirely of children and led by a charismatic leader credited as Commandant. As you get to witness the conflict through the child's eyes, his own development and his commander's, the film unfolds as an exploration of the never ending state of war in Africa. It takes you to varying conclusions, most of which you will have trouble admitting you've reached. As Commandant, Idris Elba is transfixing, and the whole cast of almost entirely non-actors, as well as the deeply authentic staging by True Detective and Sin Nombre director Cary Fukunaga, are enthralling.

WATCH IT IF IN THE MOOD FOR SOMETHING:
Humane, Intense, Raw, Thought-provoking, Touching, Well-acted

RATING:
Not Rated

LANGUAGE:
English

STARRING:
Abraham Attah, Emmanuel Affadzi, Ricky Adelayitor

WRITTEN BY:
Cary Joji Fukunaga

DIRECTED BY:
Cary Fukunaga

DRAMA | **THE ORIGINALS** | 27

Tallulah 2016

★★★☆☆

There are some actors you feel you see a lot of until a role comes by that makes you think they are actually underused. That's Ellen Page's role as Tallulah, a young girl with seemingly little regard for anyone but herself. Travelling the country while living in a van with her boyfriend; with no one to turn to or any idea how to manage such a situation, she comes across a toddler abandoned by her mother. Inevitably, she takes her in. Page, who is also the executive producer of the film, shines through the character oriented script and direction by first-timer Sian Heder. A beautiful movie.

WATCH IT IF IN THE MOOD FOR SOMETHING:
Beautiful, Character-driven, Depressing

RATING:
Not Rated

LANGUAGE:
English

STARRING:
Allison Janney, Ellen Page, Tammy Blanchard

WRITTEN BY:
Sian Heder

DIRECTED BY:
Sian Heder

DRAMA | **THE SUGGESTIONS** | 28

45 Years 2015

★★★★☆

Charlotte Rampling and Tom Courtenay both won Berlinale Best Actress and Best Actor for this movie. They play a couple who are only a few days away from their 45th marriage anniversary when they learn that the remains of the husband's first lover have been found. He then starts obsessing about his previous relationship, to the extent that when the day of the anniversary comes, there might not be a marriage left to celebrate. This is a very 'adult' movie – it's quiet, sometimes slow, very well-executed, and overall a fascinating look at marriage.

WATCH IT IF IN THE MOOD FOR SOMETHING:
A-list actors, Slow, Thought-provoking

RATING:
R

LANGUAGE:
English

STARRING:
Charlotte Rampling, Geraldine James, Tom Courtenay

WRITTEN BY:
Andrew Haigh, David Constantine

DIRECTED BY:
Andrew Haigh

DRAMA | **THE SUGGESTIONS** | 29

The Reader 2008

★★★★☆

The Reader is a German-American drama from 2008, based on the best-selling novel by author Bernhard Schlink. The storyline begins with adult Michael (Ralph Fiennes) reminiscing about his adolescence in post-World War II Berlin and his fateful relationship with an older woman named Hannah (Kate Winslet). 15-year old Michael is beset by Scarlet Fever and helped off the street one day by Hannah. Taken into her care, they soon begin a passionate affair, quickly forsaking family and friends for every opportunity to ensconce themselves in a world of lust and desire. As their time together progresses, Hannah begins urging Michael to read to her daily—to which he draws from many classic novels and delights in their rich interchange.

Hannah suddenly disappears from Michael's life, however, only reappearing several years later when young law student Michael is stunned to find her facing a World War II war-crimes tribunal. Tied to a real-life series of trials against former Auschwitz employees, The Reader is a strikingly original and exceptionally well-made film that is recommended to those who appreciate sophisticated, emotionally mannered cinema.

WATCH IT IF IN THE MOOD FOR SOMETHING:
A-list actors, Depressing

RATING:
MPAA R

LANGUAGE:
English, German

STARRING:
Bruno Ganz, Kate Winslet, Ralph Fiennes

WRITTEN BY:
David Hare

DIRECTED BY:
Stephen Daldry

DRAMA | **THE SUGGESTIONS** | 30

Divines 2016

★★★★☆

Deep in the suburbs of Paris, Divines follows the story of Dounia (played by Oulaya Amamra) and her best friend Maimouna (played by Déborah Lukumuena). Director Houda Benyamina serves a nest of social issues – welcoming the viewer into a world where poverty is pervasive and adults are haunted by their own ghosts, where there is a life vest only in the reliance on friendship. The nature of this bond between the two female characters is deep, playful, and backed by mesmerizing acting on behalf of Amamra and Lukumuena.

Just as prevailing throughout the film is the commentary on immigrant diasporas and the power of idealization. The girls fantasize about financial excess with guttural determination, guided only by the realization that their escape from their current lives has to come to fruition no matter what the cost. This film is entrancing and thought-provoking. You won't be able to look away.

WATCH IT IF IN THE MOOD FOR SOMETHING:
Character-driven

RATING:
Not Rated

LANGUAGE:
French

STARRING:
Déborah Lukumuena, Kevin Mischel, Oulaya Amamra

WRITTEN BY:
Houda Benyamina

DIRECTED BY:
Uda Benyamina

DRAMA | THE SUGGESTIONS | 31

Little Women 1994

★★★☆☆

The 1868 semi-autobiographical novels of Louisa May Alcott have been adapted into film, television and theatre so many times: 6 movies, 4 TV shows, even a broadway musical. It's a compelling story to watch as it unfolds, and it's easy to see why many hold this one as the best adaptation of the novels. For one, the cast is top-notch and perfect for the roles: Christian Bale as Laurie, Susan Sarandon as Mrs. March, and Winona Ryder, Trini Alvarado, Claire Danes and a very young Kirsten Dunst as the four sisters.

Little Women is the story of these four girls living in post-civil war America. We watch them grow together, find love, have their little fights, and try to find their place in the world. Everything from the costumes and settings to the dialogue do an excellent job of conveying the heartwarming story and the emotional impact behind it.

WATCH IT IF IN THE MOOD FOR SOMETHING:
90's-themed, Beautiful, Heart-warming

RATING:
G

LANGUAGE:
English

STARRING:
Kirsten Dunst, Susan Sarandon, Winona Ryder

WRITTEN BY:
Robin Swicord

DIRECTED BY:
Gillian Armstrong

DRAMA | **THE SUGGESTIONS** | 32

A War 2015

★★★★☆

A War (Krigen) is a Danish war drama that focuses on Commander Claus Pedersen (Pilou Asbæk) as he leads a company of soldiers in modern day Afghanistan, while his wife at home in Denmark struggles to care for their three children. During a mission to rescue a family from Taliban threat, Claus' unit is overcome by enemy fire, forcing him to make a dramatic decision that has a complicated effect upon himself, his fellow soldiers, and his family back home. A War is a tense yet thoroughly involving drama that offers a profound example of moral ambiguity and the repercussions of warfare. The acting and direction are utterly superb across the board—another enthralling and superbly humanistic affair from Danish filmmaker Tobias Lindholm (A Hijacking).

WATCH IT IF IN THE MOOD FOR SOMETHING:
Intense

RATING:
R

LANGUAGE:
Danish

STARRING:
Alex Høgh Andersen, Pilou Asbæk, Tuva Novotny

WRITTEN BY:
Tobias Lindholm

DIRECTED BY:
Tobias Lindholm

DRAMA | **THE SUGGESTIONS** | 33

Omar 2013

★★☆☆☆

Ask yourself how many Palestinian movies you have seen before. You will want to give this smart and twisty Academy Award nominee by Golden Globe winning director Hany Abu-Assad a chance to change your answer. Omar, a Palestinian baker, climbs the West Bank Wall to see his lover, Nadia, whom he wants to marry. When Israeli soldiers catch and humiliate him, he gets implicated in the shooting of an Israeli soldier, and eventually gets arrested and faces an extremely lengthy sentence. Later, his captors' motives and his own get tangled up in politics, friendship, trust, and love. Omar is a highly realistic, compelling crime drama you don't want to miss.

WATCH IT IF IN THE MOOD FOR SOMETHING:
Gripping, Raw, Thought-provoking

RATING:
Unrated

LANGUAGE:
Arabic

STARRING:
Adam Bakri, Eyad Hourani, Leem Lubany

WRITTEN BY:
Hany Abu-Assad

DIRECTED BY:
Hany Abu-Assad

DRAMA | **THE SUGGESTIONS** | 34

Breathe 2014

★★★★☆

Mélanie Laurent's fifth movie that she both directs and writes, Breathe is an impressive display of deft filmmaking and honest, insightful storytelling. Charlie is a teenage high school student with seemingly nothing unusual about her. When Sarah comes to her school from Nigeria they quickly form a friendship that brings out many unexpected sides of Charlie. Breathe sometimes veers to darkness which adds the last element to a perfect portrayal of friendship between two teenage girls.

WATCH IT IF IN THE MOOD FOR SOMETHING:
Absorbing, Humane, Touching

RATING:
Unrated

LANGUAGE:
French

STARRING:
Isabelle Carré, Joséphine Japy, Lou de Laâge

WRITTEN BY:
Anne-Sophie Brasme, Julien Lambroschini

DIRECTED BY:
Mélanie Laurent

DRAMA | **THE SUGGESTIONS** | 35

Carol 2015

★★★☆☆

Watching Carol is like reading a really interesting book while relaxing on a Sunday afternoon. It is one of those movies that you probably heard about during its Oscar run, and have since delayed actually viewing it. Well now that it is on Netflix and other streaming services you have no excuse! It's refreshingly unique, incredibly charming, and features a kind of story that hasn't been told very often – a love story between two women. Both characters played by Cate Blanchett and Rooney Mara attempt to live true to their own principles while facing unjust yet severe backlash from society. If you are open to it, the love story in this will stay with you forever.

WATCH IT IF IN THE MOOD FOR SOMETHING:
A-list actors, Beautiful, Classy, Grown-up Romance, Sunday

RATING:
R

LANGUAGE:
English

STARRING:
Cate Blanchett, Rooney Mara, Sarah Paulson

WRITTEN BY:
Patricia Highsmith, Phyllis Nagy

DIRECTED BY:
Todd Haynes

DRAMA | **THE SUGGESTIONS** | 36

Sunshine Cleaning 2008

★★★★☆

Sunshine Cleaning is a great addition to that unidentified genre of grown-up comedies populated by other great entries like Your Sister's Sister and Enough Said. It is however, less of a comedy than it is a heart-warming emotional tale. Powered by outstanding performances from Amy Adams and Emily Blunt, it ultimately evolves into a character study of failed potential and validation seeking.

Sunshine Cleaning is enjoyable, satisfying to a fault, and provides an interesting peak into the lives of its characters.

WATCH IT IF IN THE MOOD FOR SOMETHING:
Dramatic, Emotional, Grown-up Comedy, Heart-warming, Lovely, Simple

RATING:
R

LANGUAGE:
English

STARRING:
Alan Arkin, Amy Adams, Emily Blunt

WRITTEN BY:
Megan Holley

DIRECTED BY:
Christine Jeffs

DRAMA | **THE SUGGESTIONS** | 37

It's Only the End of the World 2016

★★★☆☆

Based on a play and taking place in the span of one afternoon, It's Only the End of the World is about a successful writer returning to his hometown in rural Canada baring life-altering news. But before he can share anything, he is faced with the remnants of his life prior to moving out and his family members' eccentric, but relatable, personalities. This is a movie by one of the most interesting directors working today, Canadian Xavier Dolan. Contrary to his plot-heavy Mommy (which earned him the Cannes Jury Prize at 25 years old), in It's Only the End of the World the story unfolds in a far more important way. It's an exploration of dynamics: between brother and sister, between son and mother, between brothers, etc. Don't go into it expecting things to happen, or waiting for what will happen in the end. Instead, the purpose of this film can be found in how Xavier Dolan handles his usual themes of family through big talent: Mario Cotillard, Vincent Cassel, and Léa Seydoux among many others.

WATCH IT IF IN THE MOOD FOR SOMETHING:
Dramatic, Emotional, Humane, Well-acted

RATING:
Not Rated

LANGUAGE:
French

STARRING:
Gaspard Ulliel, Léa Seydoux, Marion Cotillard, Nathalie Baye, Vincent Cassel

WRITTEN BY:
Xavier Dolan

DIRECTED BY:
Xavier Dolan

DRAMA | **THE SUGGESTIONS** | 38

Camp X-ray 2014

★★★★☆

This is Kristen Stewart's proof that she is more than a lip-biting, vampire-loving teenager. Reactive and emotive, she will not disappoint you here. Rather, expect an electrifying and exceptional performance. Paired with Payman Moaadi, they both make of this work an emotionally poignant movie that questions the notion of freedom in the unlikeliest of places: Guantanamo Bay.

WATCH IT IF IN THE MOOD FOR SOMETHING:
Absorbing, Challenging, Character-driven, Humane

RATING:
MPAA R

LANGUAGE:
English

STARRING:
Kristen Stewart, Lane Garrison, Peyman Moaadi

WRITTEN BY:
Peter Sattler

DIRECTED BY:
Peter Sattler

DRAMA | **THE SUGGESTIONS** | 39

Boyhood 2014

★★★★★

A masterpiece in every possible way: its striking balance between simplicity and effectiveness, its innovative value, the commitment of its maker, and just overall beauty. Boyhood was filmed over a span of 12 years, something never attempted before in film. The result is a captivating, breathtaking tale with almost unparalleled plausibility. The emotions it incites as well as the natural flow it has will feel a lot like life itself, and will leave you with ideas you can dwell on for long after the credits roll. Directed by Richard Linklater, and nominated for 6 different Oscars.

WATCH IT IF IN THE MOOD FOR SOMETHING:
Absorbing, Beautiful, Charming, Cute, Dramatic, Emotional, Gripping, Heart-warming, Humane, Lovely, Sincere, Thought-provoking, Warm

RATING:
MPAA R

LANGUAGE:
English

STARRING:
Ellar Coltrane, Ethan Hawke, Patricia Arquette

WRITTEN BY:
Richard Linklater

DIRECTED BY:
Richard Linklater

DRAMA | **THE SUGGESTIONS** | 40

The Founder 2016

★★★★★

Michael Keaton is the founder of McDonald's. Well, not exactly, because this movie is the story of how the man he plays, Ray Kroc, took over the company from two very innovative brothers named Mac and Dick. Played by John Carroll Lynch and none other than Nick Offerman, the brothers put up a fight while Kroc works to franchise the name and make it into a billion-dollar empire. It's a real-life story of the pursuit of the American dream through both persistence and ruthlessness, retracing Kroc's history from a struggling salesman to a fiercely pragmatic business giant. A crazy story and a cautionary tale of sorts, this is a movie that showcases America for what it is.

WATCH IT IF IN THE MOOD FOR SOMETHING:
true-story-based, Well-acted

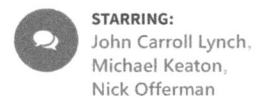

RATING:
PG-13

LANGUAGE:
English

STARRING:
John Carroll Lynch, Michael Keaton, Nick Offerman

WRITTEN BY:
Robert D. Siegel

DIRECTED BY:
John Lee Hancock

DRAMA | **THE SUGGESTIONS** | 41

The Place Beyond the Pines 2012

★★★★☆

The movie starts with Luke (Ryan Gosling) as a stunt driver who learns he has a newborn child. Luke wants to properly provide for him, so he turns to robbing banks. That causes conflict with the mother (Eva Mendes) and a police officer (Bradley Cooper), which ends up spanning two generations. The Place Beyond the Pines is gritty and emotional, and at the heart of it, a good take on father-son relationships and long-term consequences.

WATCH IT IF IN THE MOOD FOR SOMETHING:
A-list actors, Dramatic, Emotional, Raw

RATING:
MPAA R

LANGUAGE:
English

STARRING:
Bradley Cooper, Eva Mendes, Ryan Gosling

WRITTEN BY:
Ben Coccio, Derek Cianfrance

DIRECTED BY:
Derek Cianfrance

DRAMA | **THE SUGGESTIONS** | 42

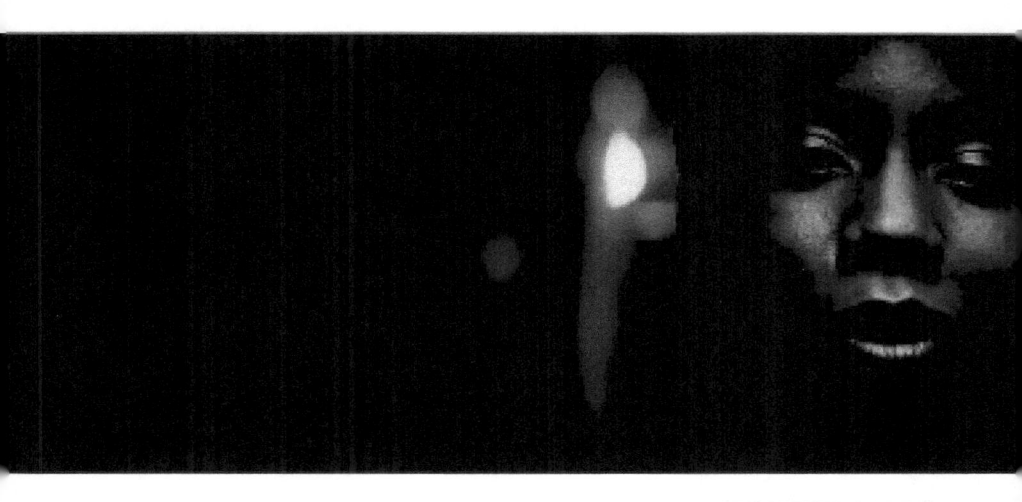

Pariah 2011

★★★☆☆

A beautiful and subtle masterpiece exploring the life of Alike, a teen in Brooklyn navigating her identity as a gay black girl. Caught between the traditional world of her family and the butch and sexual world of her friend who has already come out, director Dee Rees allows the audience to see the trials and tribulations of Alike's attempts to be comfortable and sure of herself. It's a moving and raw coming-of-age story with many characters in the film being quite lovable and relatable making it easy for the viewer to become attached.

WATCH IT IF IN THE MOOD FOR SOMETHING:
Beautiful, Character-driven, Dramatic

RATING:
R

LANGUAGE:
English

STARRING:
Aasha Davis,
Adepero Oduye,
Kim Wayans

WRITTEN BY:
Dee Rees

DIRECTED BY:
Dee Rees

DRAMA | **THE SUGGESTIONS** | 43

Half Nelson 2006

★★★★☆

The self destructive, substance abusing history teacher Dan (Ryan Gosling) works in a Brooklyn middle-school and is constantly at odds with the curriculum, preferring to teach 13 year old kids Marxist theory in class. Meanwhile, his student Drey (Shareeka Epps) has to go through struggles of her own, her brother being in jail on drug charges and her single mother having to work long hours to make ends meet. Slowly, an unlikely and tender friendship between teacher and student evolves, in which it becomes less and less clear who of them is the adult part. Steering away from cliches, Half Neslon is not your typical social drama. Its intelligent plot twists, great cast (with outstanding performances by both Gossling and Epps) and slow, non dramatic storytelling makes this a highly underestimated movie that, although treating depressive topics without any easy relief for the viewer, will leave with an inner smile, albeit a sad one.

WATCH IT IF IN THE MOOD FOR SOMETHING:
Character-driven, Humane, Well-acted

RATING:
MPAA R

LANGUAGE:
English

STARRING:
Anthony Mackie, Ryan Gosling, Shareeka Epps

WRITTEN BY:
Anna Boden, Ryan Fleck

DIRECTED BY:
Ryan Fleck

Documentary

DOCUMENTARY | **THE VERY BEST** | 44

George Harrison: Living in the Material World 2011

★★★★★

The story of one of the most influential musicians of recent history, George Harrison, told through the eyes of one of the most prominent filmmakers, Martin Scorsese. Director and producer, Scorsese offers one of the most complete documentaries on any artist – ever. And what an artist he was – successful and talented, yes, but also incredibly inspired and spiritual. Through interviews, home movies, and concert footage, this long and intimate film will allow you to travel through the world of The Beatles, and explore the incredible mind of George Harrison. A heartfelt documentary.

WATCH IT IF IN THE MOOD FOR SOMETHING:
Cool, long, Sunday

RATING:
Not Rated

LANGUAGE:
English

STARRING:
George Harrison

DIRECTED BY:
Martin Scorsese

DOCUMENTARY | **THE VERY BEST** | 45

Chasing Ice 2012

★★★★★

Incredible footage combined with a great soundtrack will keep you frozen in your seat until global warming melts you off (so to speak). Chasing Ice is about a National Geographic photographer who tries to capture a complete overview of what climate change is doing to our planet. Consequently this movie took years to make and countless technical issues had to be dealt with in order to record the time-lapse videos. The result is mesmerizing, and captures something that has never been caught on camera before. This movie is evidence of what our planet is going through that everyone can relate to. Be prepared to be charmed and saddened at the same time.

WATCH IT IF IN THE MOOD FOR SOMETHING:
Beautiful, Intense, Thought-provoking

RATING:
PG-13

LANGUAGE:
English

STARRING:
James Balog, Louie Psihoyos, Svavar Jónatansson

WRITTEN BY:
Mark Monroe

DIRECTED BY:
Jeff Orlowski

DOCUMENTARY | **THE VERY BEST** | 46

13th 2016

★★★★★

From Selma director Ava DuVernay, 13th addresses the second clause of the 13th amendment: "Neither slavery nor involuntary servitude, except as a punishment for crime whereof the party shall have been duly convicted, shall exist within the United States." A clause that was immediately exploited and for which the consequences and interpretations explain a significant part of the current American societal landscape. What also unfolds is a highly instructive and thought-provoking film that deals with the idea of progress, and justly pays tribute to the horrifying number of lives mass criminalization ruined.

WATCH IT IF IN THE MOOD FOR SOMETHING:
Instructive, Intense, Sunday, Thought-provoking

RATING:
Not Rated

LANGUAGE:
English

STARRING:
Cory Booker,
Melina Abdullah,
Michelle Alexander

WRITTEN BY:
Ava DuVernay,
Spencer Averick

DIRECTED BY:
Ava DuVernay

DOCUMENTARY | **THE VERY BEST** | 47

Blackfish 2013

★★★★★

A striking and revelatory documentary focused on the behaviour of captive Orcas and their treatment within SeaWorld and other theme parks around the world. At the center of the story is Tilikum, a bull Orca that has been responsible for the death of three individuals, and the legal and ethical challenges that have arisen from apparent cover-ups by officials. What happened to Tilikum to make him adopt such behavior? First-hand accounts by former whale trainers and experts deliver fascinating truths about Tilikum and the species as whole, with particular attention on their remarkable intelligence and advanced social behaviors. Blackfish will undoubtedly change your perspective on whale captivity indefinitely. It's certainly not to be missed by anyone who appreciates top-notch documentary film-making as honest historical record.

WATCH IT IF IN THE MOOD FOR SOMETHING:
Challenging, Thought-provoking

RATING:
PG-13

LANGUAGE:
English

WRITTEN BY:
Eli B. Despres, Gabriela Cowperthwaite

DIRECTED BY:
Gabriela Cowperthwaite

DOCUMENTARY | **THE VERY BEST** | 48

Virunga 2014

★★★★☆

A documentary that is immediate and plays out like a thriller. Beautifully shot in Virunga National Park in the Eastern Congo, the story focuses on the struggles between Park Rangers and a list of adversaries including poachers, oil company goons, and an Islamic revolutionary army. The stories of the endangered gorillas and the people who struggle to protect them will break your heart and at the same time give you hope in humanity. On top of this, the editing is superb and gives the film an intensity that rivals any recent thriller.

WATCH IT IF IN THE MOOD FOR SOMETHING:
Absorbing, Humane, Instructive, Raw, Thought-provoking

RATING:
MPAA Not Rated

LANGUAGE:
English

STARRING:
André Bauma, Emmanuel de Merode, Mélanie Gouby

WRITTEN BY:
Orlando von Einsiedel

DIRECTED BY:
Orlando von Einsiedel

DOCUMENTARY | **THE VERY BEST** | 49

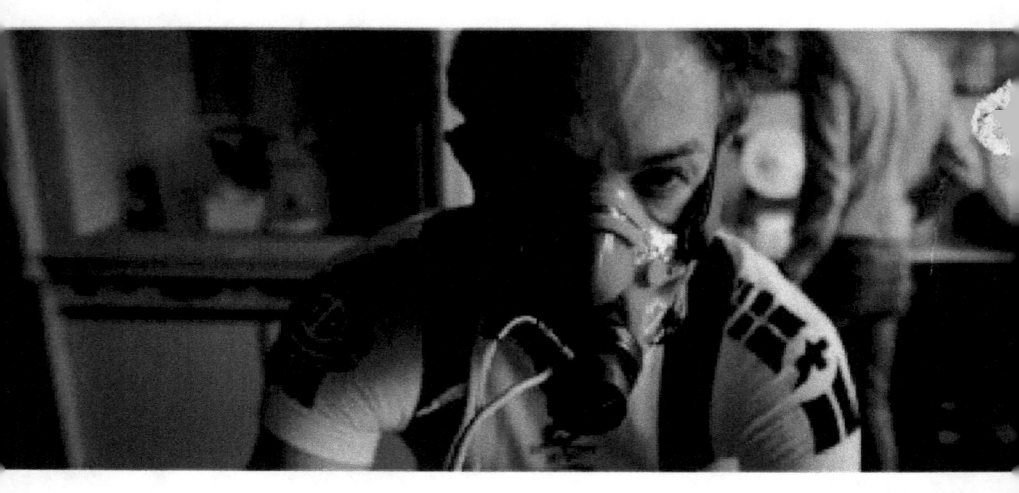

Icarus 2017

★★★★★

Icarus starts with director Bryan Fogel deciding to inject himself with doping substances and participate in a biking race undetected. By accident, he ends up in contact with a Russian scientist. This man transforms the movie from a personal experiment to a highly relevant political thriller. Dr. Grigory Rodchenkov, the scientist is at the center of accusations in Russia of a virtually impossible state-sponsored doping scheme. With links to the Russian president Putin himself, the movie keeps getting more and more interesting as the relationship between Fogel and Rodchenkov develops. Aside from all the madness that unfolds, Rodchenkov's likeable personality makes the story more relatable and humane, and gives an insight into the pressures of working in the regulatory body in a country like Russia. You will be astonished by how much material this movie has. A must-watch.

WATCH IT IF IN THE MOOD FOR SOMETHING:
Dark, Gripping, Suspenseful, Thought-provoking, Thrilling, True-crime

RATING:
TV-MA

LANGUAGE:
English

DIRECTED BY:
Bryan Fogel

DOCUMENTARY | **THE VERY BEST** | 50

Exit Through The Gift Shop 2010

★★★★★

What happens when Banksy, one of the most famous ambassadors of street art, meets Mr. Brainwash, an egocentric aspiring French artist? Well, one of the funniest, interesting and exciting documentaries ever made about art, commercialism and the apparent gulf between them. But is it really a documentary? This confident and zany film will leave you guessing.

WATCH IT IF IN THE MOOD FOR SOMETHING:
Absorbing, Fascinating, Funny, Original, Smart

RATING:
R

LANGUAGE:
English

STARRING:
Banksy, Mr. Brainwash, Space Invader

DIRECTED BY:
Banksy

DOCUMENTARY | **THE VERY BEST** | 51

The Ivory Game 2016

★★★★☆

As the value of ivory appreciated by the Chinese middle-class, the demand for it has skyrocketed. This brought elephants to a dire outlook: extinction in as early as the next 15 years. "Traders in ivory actually want extension in elephants, the less elephants there are the more the price rises" as one of the commentators in the film says. To bring awareness to this threat, filmmakers went undercover for 16 months and followed the ivory from where it was stolen to where it hits the shelves of Hong Kong. The result is a genuine thriller, far more gripping than you'd expect from a documentary. It portrays the brave and hopeful men and women trying to combat these atrocities, the battle they may be losing, and all the obstacles they face. An extremely important watch.

WATCH IT IF IN THE MOOD FOR SOMETHING:
Instructive, Thought-provoking

RATING:
MPAA Not Rated

LANGUAGE:
English

STARRING:
Andrea Crosta, Ian Stevenson, Prince William

DIRECTED BY:
Kief Davidson, Richard Ladkani

DOCUMENTARY | **THE VERY BEST** | 52

Encounters at the End of the World 2007

★★★★☆

A film by legendary director Werner Herzog where he travels to Antarctica, or rather you travel with him to study the people, the places, and the wild life of the South Pole. And when I say people I mean scientists and researchers but also truck drivers, plummers, and basically everyone with an interesting dream. This is a film for all curious minds, whether suit-trapped in a big city or out there in contact with nature every day. It's a combination so deep of unbelievable scenery and tangible sequences, that it almost becomes intangible, almost a religious experience.

WATCH IT IF IN THE MOOD FOR SOMETHING:
Beautiful, Gripping, Humane, Sunday, Thought-provoking

RATING:
MPAA G

LANGUAGE:
English

STARRING:
Scott Rowland, Stefan Pashov, Werner Herzog

WRITTEN BY:
Werner Herzog

DIRECTED BY:
Werner Herzog

DOCUMENTARY | **THE VERY BEST** | 53

Requiem for the American Dream 2015

★★★★★

On par with the best documentaries of the 21st Century thus far, "Requiem for the American Dream" is an essential viewing for the discerning viewer in search of a more complete understanding of how American society has evolved to such a dramatic point of polarization, and how both politics and big business have played a role in this process. In his introductory remarks to the film, celebrated intellectual and linguistics professor Noam Chomsky expounds: "Inequality has highly negative consequences on society as a whole, because the very fact of inequality has a corrosive, harmful effect on democracy." Chomsky spells out his perspective regarding the modern political machine and the downfall of democracy, with a keen eye to the historical decisions and influences that have sabotaged the "common good" and shaped America's current political, financial and social landscape.

WATCH IT IF IN THE MOOD FOR SOMETHING:
Instructive

RATING:
MPAA | Not Rated

LANGUAGE:
English

STARRING:
Noam Chomsky

WRITTEN BY:
Kelly Nyks, Peter D. Hutchison

DIRECTED BY:
Jared P. Scott, Kelly Nyks, Peter D. Hutchison

DOCUMENTARY | **THE VERY BEST** | 54

Jim & Andy: The Great Beyond 2017

★★★★★

When asked to play Andy Kaufman, Jim Carrey decided that he would get into character and never get out, even when the camera was not rolling. This was extremely frustrating to everyone at first, especially the director, who had no way of communicating with Jim Carrey, only Andy Kaufman or Tony Clifton (an alter ego created by Andy Kaufman). At the same time, Carrey had allowed a camera crew to follow him in order to create a behind-the-scenes documentary. The footage was never released because Universal Studios expressed concerns that "people would think Jim Carrey is an asshole". Jim & Andy is that footage being displayed for the first time since it was recorded 20 years ago, finding Carrey at a very unique point in his life. Sick of fame and almost sick of acting, he displays his true self – an unbelievably smart, fragile, and complex person. His commentary, when it's not funny impressions, is extremely emotional and grounded – sometimes philosophical. This is one of the best documentaries that Netflix has ever bought the distribution rights for, and certainly a mind-blowing portrayal of a complex mind.

WATCH IT IF IN THE MOOD FOR SOMETHING:
Dark, Emotional, Inspiring, Instructive, Smart, Sunday, Thought-provoking

RATING:
TV-MA

LANGUAGE:
English

STARRING:
Danny DeVito, Jim Carrey, Milos Forman

DIRECTED BY:
Chris Smith

DOCUMENTARY | **THE ORIGINALS** | 55

What Happened, Miss Simone? 2015

★★★★☆

"As fragile as she was strong, as vulnerable as she was dynamic, she was African royalty. How does royalty stomp around in the mud and still walk with grace?". What Happened, Miss Simone? will surprise you no matter how much you thought you knew about the soul singer – not only in its exploration of Nina Simone's personal life and complexities, but by being both a personal and political documentary. As you discover an original singer with talents that reach all the way to performance art, you will also learn about a Civil Rights activist's journey and an unstable woman's struggle. The documentary is not about answering the question of what happened, Miss Simone? – it's an exploration of why that question is so important.

WATCH IT IF IN THE MOOD FOR SOMETHING:
Emotional, Thought-provoking

RATING:
Not Rated

LANGUAGE:
English

STARRING:
James Baldwin, Stokely Carmichael, Walter Cronkite

DIRECTED BY:
Liz Garbus

DOCUMENTARY | **THE ORIGINALS** | 56

Into the Inferno 2016

★★★★☆

From countries like Finland to North Korea, this amazing documentary explores the most fascinating active volcanoes on our planet. But as it unfolds you realize that Into the Inferno is a movie as much about volcanoes as it is about the people obsessed with them. And who can be called obsessive more than the film's own director, Werner Herzog, who, with such an explosive career had to eventually make a film about volcanos (bad pun intended). Beautiful scenery, interesting interviews, and Werner's majestic delivery all make Into the Inferno both an interesting and satisfying documentary.

WATCH IT IF IN THE MOOD FOR SOMETHING:
Beautiful, Instructive

RATING:
Not Rated

LANGUAGE:
English

STARRING:
Clive Oppenheimer, Katia Krafft, Werner Herzog

WRITTEN BY:
Werner Herzog

DIRECTED BY:
Werner Herzog

DOCUMENTARY | **THE ORIGINALS** | 57

The White Helmets 2016

★★★★☆

The White Helmets, the 2016 Academy Award for Best Documentary Short Subject, is a concise but riveting documentation of the titular rescue organization that formed in Syria in 2012. Set primarily in the war-torn city of Aleppo, the film captures the day-to-day efforts of the White Helmet volunteers as they respond to the sites of airstrikes and bombings in order to remove survivors and victims from demolished buildings. Director Orlando von Einsiedel (Virunga) clearly put himself in the face of it to capture remarkable footage of war and ruin, illuminating the unimaginable destruction and death beset upon the Syrian people over the course of nearly 6 years of civil war. It's a remarkable effort, highlighted by the profound one-on-one interviews with members of The White Helmets. They each express their heartfelt desire to save the lives of other human beings, even as they yearn for peace and the safety of their own families and friends. Indeed their official credo from The Quran, as explained in the film, reads "Whoever saves one life, saves all of humanity."

WATCH IT IF IN THE MOOD FOR SOMETHING:
Challenging, Depressing, Humane, Inspiring, Thought-provoking

RATING:
MPAA TV-14

LANGUAGE:
Arabic

DOCUMENTARY | **THE SUGGESTIONS** | 58

The Look of Silence 2015

★★★★☆

The Look of Silence is an incredible documentary from Director Joshua Oppenheimer, a follow-up/companion piece to his award-winning documentary The Act of Killing. Both films focus on the Indonesian Genocide of 1965-66, where the military government systematically purged up to one million communists. In this film an optician named Adi Rukun meets with various members of the death squad that murdered his brother, under the guise of providing them eye examinations. As he questions them about their participation in the killings, they show little remorse and in fact provide lurid details to the many executions. It's a stunning and provocative look at the legacy of historical violence, along with the insidious propaganda that provoked it then and continues to justify it to younger generations.

WATCH IT IF IN THE MOOD FOR SOMETHING:
Absorbing, Challenging, Gripping, Intense, Thought-provoking, True-crime, true-story-based

RATING:
PG-13

LANGUAGE:
Indonesian

DIRECTED BY:
Joshua Oppenheimer

DOCUMENTARY | **THE SUGGESTIONS** | 59

Jiro Dreams of Sushi 2011

★★★★★

This surprising documentary follows Jiro, an 85 year old Japanese chef, his Michelin-starred restaurant in the Tokyo underground, and his eager sons. While ostensibly about sushi – and believe me, you'll learn about sushi and see absolutely gorgeous images of the raw-fish creations – the film's dramatic impetus is carried by the weight of tradition, the beauty of a labor of love, obsession, and the relationship between father and son. Truly a must-watch.

WATCH IT IF IN THE MOOD FOR SOMETHING:
Beautiful, Inspiring

RATING:
PG

LANGUAGE:
Japanese

STARRING:
Jiro Ono, Masuhiro Yamamoto, Yoshikazu Ono

DIRECTED BY:
David Gelb

DOCUMENTARY | **THE SUGGESTIONS** | 60

Twinsters 2015

★★★★☆

Twinsters is a documentary about a young Asian American actress, Samantha Futerman (also co-director), who is contacted over the internet by a young French-Asian woman, Anaïs Bordier, who has been shown a video of Samantha on the internet — and cannot believe their remarkably similar physical appearance. After initial perplexity and uncertainty, Samantha and Anaïs are soon embroiled in excited correspondence and travel to meet one another in their respective countries — eventually confirming via DNA testing that they are in fact long-lost twin sisters given up for adoption 25 years earlier in South Korea. A remarkable true story with a wonderfully beating heart, Twinsters does a lovely job of not just spelling out the amazing story of the sisters' unlikely connection, but also finding and exploring the growing love and affection between both the two girls, as well as their extended families and groups of friends. A truly touching and humanistic film-viewing experience.

WATCH IT IF IN THE MOOD FOR SOMETHING:
Beautiful, Humane, true-story-based

RATING:
PG-13

LANGUAGE:
English

STARRING:
Anaïs Bordier, Kanoa Goo, Samantha Futerman

WRITTEN BY:
Samantha Futerman

DIRECTED BY:
Ryan Miyamoto, Samantha Futerman

DOCUMENTARY | **THE SUGGESTIONS** | 61

Finding Vivian Maier 2013

★★★★☆

Vivian Maier was a French-American photographer whose art, like many of the greats, only gained widespread success after her death. Most of her life was spent working as a maid for families in Chicago. Her masterpieces were only introduced to the world when the director of this documentary purchased a box of her negatives. This movie is about him trying to put together the pieces and retrace her life by interviewing the people that knew her.

Right from the beginning of this documentary her photos will have you in awe. They gave me chills and made me feel exactly what I needed to feel to understand each photo. Cue Vivian's unexpected dark side along with really messed up backstory, I was completely absorbed. Interviews, along with Vivian's own photos and home videos show the complexity and mystery of the artist.

WATCH IT IF IN THE MOOD FOR SOMETHING:
Humane, Inspiring, Sunday

RATING:
Not Rated

LANGUAGE:
English

WRITTEN BY:
Charlie Siskel, John Maloof

DIRECTED BY:
Charlie Siskel, John Maloof

DOCUMENTARY | **THE SUGGESTIONS** | 62

Living on One Dollar 2013

★★★☆☆

An earnest, simple documentary with an equally as simple premise: four friends travel to Guatemala for 8 weeks and try to live on one dollar a day each. What starts as an experiment for them quickly becomes an illustration of levels of poverty some of us will luckily never experience. More than 1.1 billion people (almost four times the population of the U.S.) do live on less than one dollar a day, and this film is a journey into their world. Other than making you realize the luxury you live in, this film will leave you wanting to do more for your fellow humans.

WATCH IT IF IN THE MOOD FOR SOMETHING:
Humane, Inspiring, Thought-provoking

RATING:
Not Rated

LANGUAGE:
English

STARRING:
Ryan Christoffersen, Sean Leonard, Zach Ingrasci

DIRECTED BY:
Chris Temple, Sean Leonard, Zach Ingrasci

DOCUMENTARY | **THE SUGGESTIONS** | 63

Last Days in Vietnam 2014

★★★★★

Last Days in Vietnam is a documentary that recounts the final weeks of the conflict in 1975, as North Vietnamese forces surged toward Saigon and U.S personnel anxiously awaited word of an evacuation plan. At the time, U.S. Ambassador Graham Martin was reluctant to accept defeat, and delayed a U.S. withdrawal in his (rapidly diminishing) hopes that a solution could be reached. Once the fall of Saigon became imminent, U.S. diplomatic, military and intelligence personnel were left piecing together a bare bones plan to escape via military helicopter support. The moral dilemma they soon faced was the harsh reality of leaving behind so many South Vietnamese citizens who had supported the American effort—many of whom faced likely imprisonment and/or death. Featuring remarkable footage and first-hand accounts from many involved, the film recounts those final days of chaos and confusion in stunningly dramatic fashion. Director Rory Kennedy has put together a gripping and emotionally compelling film that balances broad historical exposition with concise detail related to the evacuation complexities—all of it punctuated by remarkable examples of bravery and heroism.

WATCH IT IF IN THE MOOD FOR SOMETHING:
Absorbing, Inspiring, Instructive, Thought-provoking

RATING:
Not Rated

LANGUAGE:
English

WRITTEN BY:
Keven McAlester, Mark Bailey

DIRECTED BY:
Rory Kennedy

DOCUMENTARY | **THE SUGGESTIONS** | 64

Man on Wire 2008

★★★★☆

Man on Wire is a true technical masterpiece. You can almost feel the director telling the cameraman what angle to choose, or thinking about the questions that will generate the most resounding answers. However, this does not diminish the story this documentary tells one bit. It's one that is glorious, riveting, and fun. It's one where you feel like an insider to a world lived on and below wires, with high-stake risks. Hopefully the edge of your seat is comfortable, because this is where the movie will keep you till the very end.

WATCH IT IF IN THE MOOD FOR SOMETHING:
Absorbing, Inspiring, Thrilling, true-story-based, Uplifting

RATING:
PG-13

LANGUAGE:
English

STARRING:
Jean François Heckel, Jean-Louis Blondeau, Philippe Petit

WRITTEN BY:
Philippe Petit

DIRECTED BY:
James Marsh

DOCUMENTARY | **THE SUGGESTIONS** | 65

Joan Didion: The Center Will Not Hold 2017

★★★★★

The Centre Will Not Hold explores the life of the famous Joan Didion – professional observer and cultural spectator. The film gives only a small window into the complexity of her mind and the space in which she processes and understands the world, which stems from her capacity to sit above everything that is happening around her and just observe. From writing for Vogue, to war journalism, to her famous novels – from watching a child do acid, to reporting on the first gulf war – Didion is as prolific as she is insightful and majestic in her writing. Throughout the documentary she gives her first hand perspectives on love, relationships, motherhood, and grief – beautifully articulating it as "a place we do not know unless we've been there." A beautiful woman, and an incredible film.

WATCH IT IF IN THE MOOD FOR SOMETHING:
Beautiful, Instructive, Thought-provoking

RATING:
Not Rated

LANGUAGE:
English

STARRING:
Dick Cheney, Hilton Als, Tom Brokaw

DIRECTED BY:
Griffin Dunne

DOCUMENTARY | **THE SUGGESTIONS** | 66

Ai Weiwei: Never Sorry

2012

★★★★☆

An inspiring documentary about famed artist Ai Weiwei who has been the source of arguably the biggest public confrontation with the Chinese government by any artist. His straightforward attitude is made to provoke and to defend the people of China against the totalitarian regime. The film portrays Weiwei's very visible struggle for redemption and invoke a sense of accountability from the government. The documentary is also about him as a person, his intimate relationships and his interactions with his family as he prepares for a big exhibition. A rare insight into a fascinating mind.

WATCH IT IF IN THE MOOD FOR SOMETHING:
Depressing, long, Thought-provoking

RATING:
MPAA R

LANGUAGE:
English, Mandarin

STARRING:
Ai Weiwei

WRITTEN BY:
Alison Klayman

DIRECTED BY:
Alison Klayman

DOCUMENTARY | **THE SUGGESTIONS** | 67

How to Change the World 2015

★★★★★

How to Change the World is an insightful and candid documentary about the formation of Greenpeace in 1971 by a small group of environmentalists and activists in Vancouver, British Columbia. Beginning with their attempt to disrupt U.S. nuclear testing in Amchitka, Alaska, the film follows their subsequent efforts to thwart commercial whaling in the Pacific, their anti-sealing campaign in Newfoundland, and their ongoing efforts to defend the natural world against what they perceive as excessive human intervention and abuse. How to Change the World is as much a poignant tale of inspired activism as it is an interesting study of the organization's early tribulations: idealism vs. anarchy, social movement vs. organizational structure (or lack thereof) and leadership vs. disunity. The voice of co-founder Robert Hunter (de facto leader of Greenpeace from inception) is heard posthumously throughout via narrator Barry Pepper, and it adds an impassioned air of gravitas to the film, detailing the many complexities Greenpeace experienced over the course of its early years of growth and development. A compelling and educational viewing experience.

WATCH IT IF IN THE MOOD FOR SOMETHING:
Inspiring, Instructive

RATING:
Not Rated

LANGUAGE:
English

STARRING:
Bill Darnell, Bobbi Hunter, David Garrick

WRITTEN BY:
Jerry Rothwell

DIRECTED BY:
Jerry Rothwell

DOCUMENTARY | **THE SUGGESTIONS** | 68

Welcome to Leith 2015

★★★★★

At first glance, one may think that Welcome to Leith is a well thought-out fictional thriller of people's most unwarranted night terrors. But if you squint real hard, you will come to realize that it portrays a scary reality in which violence, fear, and isolation is prevalent and that it could happen to possibly any town with little to no effort. Nichols and Walker aim to capture this frightening message in hopes of bringing awareness, using white supremacist Craig Cobb's attempt at taking over the small North Dakotan town to display objectivity in an otherwise touchy subject.

WATCH IT IF IN THE MOOD FOR SOMETHING:
Challenging, Intense, True-crime

RATING:
Not Rated

LANGUAGE:
English

WRITTEN BY:
Christopher K. Walker, Michael Beach Nichols

DIRECTED BY:
Christopher K. Walker, Michael Beach Nichols

DOCUMENTARY | **THE SUGGESTIONS** | 69

Food, Inc 2008

★★★☆☆

An equally interesting and terrifying must-watch documentary about the state of food in the United States, Food Inc is a sobering tour of where the stuff you eat comes from. Spoiler alert: it's gross, and should be illegal but that shouldn't stop you from watching this film, which showcases the food industry's vile practices and overt corruption. Don't worry though, even at its most muckraking, Food Inc manages to mix entertainment with its information.

WATCH IT IF IN THE MOOD FOR SOMETHING:
Depressing, Instructive

RATING:
PG

LANGUAGE:
English

STARRING:
Eric Schlosser, Michael Pollan, Richard Lobb

WRITTEN BY:
Elise Pearlstein, Robert Kenner

DIRECTED BY:
Robert Kenner

DOCUMENTARY | **THE SUGGESTIONS** | 70

Unrest 2017

★★★★★

A deeply affecting and meaningful documentary, directed by the woman who it revolves around. Jennifer Brea, a Harvard Ph.D student, begins suffering from unusual symptoms: prolonged and extreme fatigue, mental confusion, full-body pain, etc. When she goes to the doctor she is dismissed for being dehydrated and depressed. Later she finds an extended community suffering from her exact same symptoms, all of which fall under the umbrella of Myalgic Encephalomyelitis, more widely known as Chronic Fatigue Syndrome. She decides to tell their stories from her bed, and as such this movie is a collection of videos from her and her partner, added to the stories of others living with the disease. An important and inspiring movie that sheds a light on the lives of the millions affected by CFS around the world. Watch the trailer.

WATCH IT IF IN THE MOOD FOR SOMETHING:
Humane, Inspiring, Instructive, Sunday

RATING:
Not Rated

LANGUAGE:
English

STARRING:
Jennifer Brea, Jessica I e Taylor, Omar Wasow

WRITTEN BY:
Jennifer Brea, Kim Roberts

DIRECTED BY:
Jennifer Brea

DOCUMENTARY | THE SUGGESTIONS | 71

Undefeated 2011

★★★★☆

Undefeated won an Oscar but since it's a documentary, few sadly paid attention to it. It tells the story of a football team in a poor area in Tennessee. Kids without a bright future, until the new coach arrives. Yes, that sounds like a very old, cliché tale. But keep in mind it is a documentary, and the story it tells is powerful, gripping, and any familiarity quickly becomes irrelevant. Even if you have no interest in American football, or in sports in general, you will love it and more than likely find yourself reaching for the Kleenex at least a few times before the credits roll.

WATCH IT IF IN THE MOOD FOR SOMETHING:
Emotional, Gripping, Sunday

RATING:
PG-13

LANGUAGE:
English

STARRING:
Bill Courtney, Montrail 'Money' Brown, O.C. Brown

DIRECTED BY:
Daniel Lindsay, T. J. Martin

DOCUMENTARY | **THE SUGGESTIONS** | 72

Under the Sun 2015

★★★☆☆

When Russian director Vitaly Mansky is commissioned by the North Korean government to make a documentary about an average Pyongyang child, he follows their every guideline. Except the end result, Under The Sun, is the complete opposite of what they had intended. For example starting every take earlier than they thought, he makes the documentary about the watchdogs around the child and other mechanisms of propaganda. He uses quiet storytelling to expose how brainwashing in a fascist regime takes place, and how the people caught in it function. May just be the smartest, most important film you can watch on North Korea.

WATCH IT IF IN THE MOOD FOR SOMETHING:
Humane, Instructive, Thought-provoking

RATING:
Not Rated

LANGUAGE:
English, Korean

STARRING:
Hye-Yong, Lee Zin-Mi, Yu-Yong

WRITTEN BY:
Vitaliy Manskiy

DIRECTED BY:
Vitaly Mansky

Horror

HORROR | **THE VERY BEST** | 73

It Follows 2014

★★★★★

This movie is distilled horror. A teenager sleeps with her boyfriend for the first time, after which he tells her that he was the latest recipient of a curse that is transmitted through sexual contact. After she becomes completely paranoid without any manifestations, the curse manifests itself in assassins that kill their way to her. A genuinely creepy film that's also very smart.

WATCH IT IF IN THE MOOD FOR SOMETHING:
Gripping, Raw

RATING:
R

LANGUAGE:
English

STARRING:
Keir Gilchrist, Maika Monroe, Olivia Luccardi

WRITTEN BY:
David Robert Mitchell

DIRECTED BY:
David Robert Mitchell

HORROR | **THE ORIGINALS** | 74

Gerald's Game 2017

★★★☆☆

Based on the Stephen King book, this is a slow-burning horror thriller with a seemingly limited premise. Jesse and Gerald are in a house in the countryside and their attempt to spice up their relationship turns out catastrophic. Gerald suffers from a heart attack while Jesse finds herself handcuffed to a bed without the keys. The movie follows her, and at every turn blows your mind about what can be done in a movie where the main character is glued to a bed for most of the run-time. An original movie for true horror fans only, as it might seem a little too absurd and slow for anyone else.

WATCH IT IF IN THE MOOD FOR SOMETHING:
A-list actors, Intense, Raw, Weird

RATING:
TV-MA

LANGUAGE:
English

STARRING:
Bruce Greenwood, Carla Gugino, Chiara Aurelia

WRITTEN BY:
Jeff Howard, Mike Flanagan

DIRECTED BY:
Mike Flanagan

HORROR | THE SUGGESTIONS | 75

Tucker and Dale vs. Evil

2010

★★★★☆

Full of twists on classic horror themes, this hilarious and gory comedy will have your sides aching, and still you'll want more. The plot centers on two rednecks who are trying to have a good time while fixing up a summer home. True to horror movie form, a group of college kids set up camp nearby, and naturally evil begins to happen. This well-written, entertaining story even has some heart to it.

WATCH IT IF IN THE MOOD FOR SOMETHING:
Funny, Weird

RATING:
R

LANGUAGE:
English

STARRING:
Alan Tudyk, Katrina Bowden, Tyler Labine

WRITTEN BY:
Eli Craig, Morgan Jurgenson

DIRECTED BY:
Eli Craig

HORROR | **THE SUGGESTIONS** | 76

Train to Busan 2016

★★★★☆

It's disaster movie true to the guidelines of the genre, and yet with a little Korean twist it manages to be refreshingly thrilling. While a father tries to take his daughter from Seoul to Busan, the second largest city in Korea, a zombie virus breaks out. Together with other passengers they try to survive until Busan, with news coming in that it's a safe zone untouched by the virus. The acting is spot on, the set pieces are well choreographed, and most importantly it makes you care about the characters through the father's struggle to keep the governing principles of humanity in the bleakest of scenarios.

WATCH IT IF IN THE MOOD FOR SOMETHING:
Action-packed, Intense, Thrilling

RATING:
Not Rated

LANGUAGE:
Korean

STARRING:
Dong-seok Ma, Yoo Gong, Yu-mi Jung

WRITTEN BY:
Joo-Suk Park, Sang-ho Yeon

DIRECTED BY:
Sang-ho Yeon

HORROR | **THE SUGGESTIONS** | 77

The Wailing 2016

★★★★☆

In rural Korea a policeman starts to investigate peculiar and violent events that most of the people in his village attribute to the arrival of a new Japanese resident. As the occurrences keep multiplying, and different perspectives in the film are shown, you start to lose touch with reality in the face of what can only be described as genius filmmaking. As critic Jada Yuan puts it, the film operates on a level "that makes most American cinema seem clunky and unimaginative". For this reason, and while The Wailing is a true horror flick with a great premise, it's also more than just that: it boosts a mind-boggling, interesting plot that will have you thinking about it long after the credits roll. Protip: grab the person next to you and make them watch this movie with you so you can have someone to discuss it with after!

WATCH IT IF IN THE MOOD FOR SOMETHING:
Dramatic, Gripping, Mysterious, Suspenseful, Thought-provoking, Weird

RATING:
Not Rated

LANGUAGE:
Korean

STARRING:
Do-won Kwak, Jun Kunimura, Jung-min Hwang

WRITTEN BY:
Hong-jin Na

DIRECTED BY:
Hong-jin Na

HORROR | **THE SUGGESTIONS** | 78

Under the Shadow 2016

★★★★☆

Horror movies have always been creepier to me when they play on our fear of the "unknown" rather than gore. Under The Shadow does exactly that. The story is based around the relationship of a woman, Shideh, and her daughter, Dorsa, under the backdrop of the Iran-Iraq war. As widespread bombings shake the ground beneath their feet, the two grapple with a more insidious evil that is faceless and traceless, coming and going only with the wind. The movie's dread-effect plays strongly on feelings of isolation and helplessness. The scares are slow and it's obvious the director takes great care in making every single second count and in raising the unpredictableness of the action. Like the bombs, the audience never knows when or how the next apparition will materialize. The former is always on the edge of fear, wondering what is no doubt there, but is yet to be shown on the frame. In terms of significance, Under The Shadow features too many symbolisms to count and will most likely resonate with each person differently. But one thing remains relatively unarguable: this is a wonderful movie.

WATCH IT IF IN THE MOOD FOR SOMETHING:
Intense, Mysterious, Suspenseful

RATING:
MPAA PG-13

LANGUAGE:
Persian

STARRING:
Avin Manshadi, Bobby Naderi, Narges Rashidi

WRITTEN BY:
Babak Anvari

DIRECTED BY:
Babak Anvari

HORROR | **THE SUGGESTIONS** | 79

The Babadook 2014

★★★☆☆

In an age where recent horror films mostly use the jump-scare as a crutch to make their CGI-spawned (not to mention generic) creatures seem scary, The Babadook portrays real scares, relatable characters and a moving story. Jennifer Kent (director and writer) sets this on the backdrop of heavily Lars von Trier-inspired cinematography, elevating The Babadook from a shot at an amazing horror to a resemblance of an art house film. The unease felt during this film only increases as it creeps towards its conclusion. Whenever the Babadook (the monster of the film) is seen lurking in the peripherals of the camera, appearing in television sets and the shadows to create a sense of omnipresence that disturbs the viewer on a deeper, more primal level than that of so many recent horror films could even hope to reach. It leaves the audience with the sensation that they are being lowered onto a lit candle, spine-first. In short; the seamless acting, the beautiful shots, the slow-burning terror together creates a masterpiece that strides past any horror film of the past decade (maybe even further) and stands toe-to-toe with the greats without even breaking a sweat.

WATCH IT IF IN THE MOOD FOR SOMETHING:
Challenging, Thrilling

RATING:
Not Rated

LANGUAGE:
English

STARRING:
Daniel Henshall, Essie Davis, Noah Wiseman

WRITTEN BY:
Jennifer Kent

DIRECTED BY:
Jennifer Kent

Mystery

MYSTERY | **THE VERY BEST** | 80

OldBoy 2003

★★★★★

On his daughter's birthday, Oh Dae-su gets drunk and is arrested by the police. His friend bails him out of jail and while he is making a phone call Oh Dae-su disappears, and is held by unknown captors, in a room for 15 years only to see the outside world through a television. But one day he's released. That's all that can be revealed, without telling too much of this intense and twisted film. All I can add, and this is precisely how I recommend Oldboy to new viewers: "You're welcome & I'm sorry." It is truly a twisted film, one that is mesmerizing in it's directing, acting, and plot, all of which will stay with you whether you like it or not.

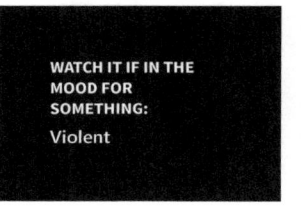

WATCH IT IF IN THE MOOD FOR SOMETHING:
Violent

RATING:
R

LANGUAGE:
Korean

STARRING:
Hye-jeong Kang, Ji-tae Yu, Min-sik Choi

WRITTEN BY:
Garon Tsuchiya

DIRECTED BY:
Park Chan-wook

MYSTERY | **THE ORIGINALS** | 81

I Don't Feel at Home in This World Anymore 2017

★★★☆☆

This is the first film directed by actor Macon Blair (so good in both Blue Ruin and Green Room), and while it is shaggy and tonally all over the place, there is a lot to recommend here. First off, I'm a huge fan of the (underrated) Melanie Lynskey, so I was primed to like this movie from the get-go. After Ruth's (Lynskey) home is broken into, she seeks revenge against the perpetrators with help from her martial arts obsessed neighbor Tony (Elijah Wood, sporting an impressive rat-tail). What starts out as an empowering journey for Ruth & Tony quickly teeters into dangerous and increasingly violent territory. This movie is probably not for everyone, but if you're a fan of 90s indie films and don't mind some violence mixed in with your dark humor, then you will enjoy this small, well-acted film.

WATCH IT IF IN THE MOOD FOR SOMETHING:
Character-driven, Dark, Funny, Original, Raw, Twisted, Unique, Violent, Weird

RATING:
Not Rated

LANGUAGE:
English

STARRING:
Chris Doubek, Marilyn Faith Hickey, Melanie Lynskey

WRITTEN BY:
Macon Blair

DIRECTED BY:
Macon Blair

MYSTERY | **THE SUGGESTIONS** | 82

The Prestige 2006

★★★★★

This movie will first confuse your perception of the narrative with a feud involving the two magicians (played by Hugh Jackman and Christian Bale), but you will soon be hooked by the twists and turns of the plot. The unveiling of the mystery will leave you in awe, however it is the storytelling and the process that Christopher Nolan puts together so beautifully that is the greatest thing about this movie.

WATCH IT IF IN THE MOOD FOR SOMETHING:
Absorbing, Challenging, Well-acted

RATING:

LANGUAGE:
English

STARRING:
Christian Bale, Hugh Jackman, Scarlett Johansson

WRITTEN BY:
Christopher Nolan, Jonathan Nolan

DIRECTED BY:
Christopher Nolan

MYSTERY | **THE SUGGESTIONS** | 83

Donnie Darko 2001

★★★★☆

Donnie Darko is a cult film by director Richard Kelly, starring Jake Gyllenhaal. It's about the troubled teenager Donnie who lives in a suburb and suddenly faces a person in a giant rabbit costume who tells him that the world is going to end in 28 days. If that didn't make sense to you, don't worry – it's not about making sense. The film is a gorgeous exploration of a bizarre chain of events, a deep rabbit-hole of meaning and expression, fate and acceptance that practically begs for a second, third, or fourth watching.

WATCH IT IF IN THE MOOD FOR SOMETHING:
Challenging, Dark, Mysterious, Original

RATING:
R

LANGUAGE:
English

STARRING:
Jake Gyllenhaal, Jena Malone, Mary McDonnell

WRITTEN BY:
Richard Kelly

DIRECTED BY:
Richard Kelly

MYSTERY | **THE SUGGESTIONS** | 84

The Best Offer 2013

★★★☆☆

A riveting take on one of the most prestigious forms of modern art, *The Best Offer* is a film laced with symbolism and thick, posh accents. Virgil Oldman (Geoffrey Rush) ends up pursuing a socially inept woman through Robert (Jim Sturgess), who guides him in winning her heart, albeit, rather unconventionally. What starts out as something Oldman brushes off to be some poor laid-out scam ends up a mystery he begins obsessing over, turning his life to shambles of sorts.

This uncanny film by Academy Award-winning director Giuseppe Tornatore delivers sharp twists and appropriately-timed surprises in a suspense-thriller served on a silver platter.

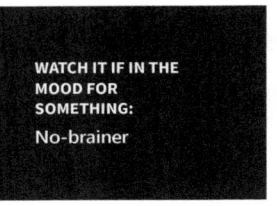

WATCH IT IF IN THE MOOD FOR SOMETHING:
No-brainer

RATING:
R

LANGUAGE:
English

STARRING:
Geoffrey Rush, Jim Sturgess, Sylvia Hoeks

WRITTEN BY:
Giuseppe Tornatore

DIRECTED BY:
Giuseppe Tornatore

MYSTERY | **THE SUGGESTIONS** | 85

The Gift 2015

★★★★☆

The Gift is Joel Edgerton's directoral debut, a twisted and smart thriller that sneaks up on you where you least expect it. He also stars in it as Gordo, a friend from the past that enters a new couple's life (played by Jason Bateman and Rebecca Hall) and brings a secret that has been hidden for decades. A very "movie" movie, it has enough in it that's original and enough that's not to make for a very enjoyable 100 minutes.

WATCH IT IF IN THE MOOD FOR SOMETHING:
A-list actors, Thrilling, Well-acted

RATING:
R

LANGUAGE:
English

STARRING:
Jason Bateman, Joel Edgerton, Rebecca Hall

WRITTEN BY:
Joel Edgerton

DIRECTED BY:
Joel Edgerton

Romance

ROMANCE | **THE VERY BEST** | 86

Blue Is the Warmest Color 2013

★★★★☆

Emma, a free-spirited girl with blue hair, influences Adele's life dramatically, teaching her how to be honest with herself and discover her true desires about love. The film beautifully and realistically portrays the Adele's evolution, from a highschool girl to a grown-up woman. The spirit Emma lights up in her never dies. Blue Is the Warmest Color or La Vie d'Adèle is an honest, intense, and charming picture, prepare not to blink and have your face glued to screen from start to finish.

WATCH IT IF IN THE MOOD FOR SOMETHING:
Absorbing, Intense, Original, Romantic, Thought-provoking

RATING:
MPAA NC-17

LANGUAGE:
French

STARRING:
Adèle Exarchopoulos, Léa Seydoux, Salim Kechiouche

WRITTEN BY:
Abdellatif Kechiche, Ghalia Lacroix

DIRECTED BY:
Abdellatif Kechiche

ROMANCE | **THE VERY BEST** | 87

On Body and Soul 2017

★★★★★

On Body and Soul is the impeccably crafted winner of the 2017 Berlin Film Festival. Two strangers have the same dream every night, they meet as deer in a forest and eventually fall in love. When they run into each other in real life and search for the love they experience once unconscious, their introverted personalities as well as their surroundings add variables that make it hard to establish that same connection. This unconventional love story is beautifully and passionately made by Hungary's best director, who had taken an 18-year break from making movies. When you watch it you will realize that her break was probably the only way someone could so creatively and tenderly make something like On Body and Soul.

WATCH IT IF IN THE MOOD FOR SOMETHING:
Absorbing, Beautiful, Grown-up Romance, Warm

RATING:
Not Rated

LANGUAGE:
Hungarian

STARRING:
Alexandra Borbély, Géza Morcsányi, Zoltán Schneider

WRITTEN BY:
Ildikó Enyedi

DIRECTED BY:
Ildikó Enyedi

ROMANCE | **THE ORIGINALS** | 88

Tramps 2016

★★★★☆

Danny (Callum Turner) is a young man struggling to make ends meet in New York. His brother, spending the night in jail, urges him to take his place in a small heist. His job is simple : He would meet Ellie (Grace Van Patten), she would drive him to take a briefcase, and then to a train station where he would exchange the briefcase with a woman holding a green purse. You've probably guessed what might go wrong in a plan like this: another woman with another green purse. Danny makes the trade quickly and, being the nervous guy that he is, storms off only to find later that he had taken the wrong briefcase. This is how Danny and Ellie's little adventure begins as they track down the woman with the green purse throughout New York.

Tramps is a simple romantic comedy filled with genuine charm that will make you fall in love with the characters, and maybe even the two first-time actors that portray them – as they slowly grow closer to each other. The lively soundtrack and engaging writing are all the more reason to watch this lovely little film.

WATCH IT IF IN THE MOOD FOR SOMETHING:
Charming, No-brainer, Romantic, Simple, Warm

RATING:
Not Rated

LANGUAGE:
English

STARRING:
Callum Turner, Grace Van Patten, Michal Vondel

WRITTEN BY:
Adam Leon

DIRECTED BY:
Adam Leon

ROMANCE | **THE SUGGESTIONS** | 89

Keith 2008

★★★☆☆

I was pleasantly surprised at how much I liked this film. I'll be honest and say I did not really expect much given that it starred Jesse McCartney in the title role. Nevertheless, he managed to really surprise me. McCartney and Harnois have excellent chemistry as Keith and Natalie and you find yourself rooting for them to end up together. The film does a great job at building up their relationship and emotional connection, and it will definitely succeed in pulling at your heartstrings. If you enjoy films in the vein of A Walk to Remember, you should check this one out!

WATCH IT IF IN THE MOOD FOR SOMETHING:
Romantic

RATING:
PG-13

LANGUAGE:
English

STARRING:
Elisabeth Harnois, Jesse McCartney, Margo Harshman

WRITTEN BY:
David Zabel, Todd Kessler

DIRECTED BY:
Todd Kessler

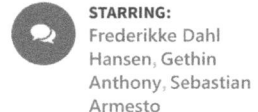

ROMANCE | **THE SUGGESTIONS** | 90

Copenhagen 2014

★★★☆☆

Though it starts off somewhat slow, I was delightfully surprised at how much I loved this movie. A 28-year-old man ventures through Europe with a buddy, ending in Copenhagen, where he hopes to contact the last of his family. There he enlists a local girl to help him. An interesting relationship unfolds as they take a captivating journey through Copenhagen in search of William's grandfather. The tag line of the movie is "When the girl of your dreams is half your age, it's time to grow up" and William really does have to grow up when he's faced with his own personal tumult.

The girl is played by Frederikke Dahl Hansen, who gives an exceptional natural performance, which adds even more to the abundance of charm in this film.

WATCH IT IF IN THE MOOD FOR SOMETHING:
Beautiful, Humane, Original, Weird

RATING:
Unrated

LANGUAGE:
Danish, English

STARRING:
Frederikke Dahl Hansen, Gethin Anthony, Sebastian Armesto

WRITTEN BY:
Mark Raso

DIRECTED BY:
Mark Raso

ROMANCE | **THE SUGGESTIONS** | 91

Y Tu Mamá También 2001

★★★★☆

Tenoch and Julio, mischievous and sex-crazed teenagers and best friends, embark from Mexico City to a remote and mythical beach with the company of an older and very attractive woman. This poetically written and directed film has it all; great acting, cultural relevancy, thought-provoking questions, and beautiful scenery. All put together by Alfonso Cuarón and his brother in star-making efforts for both of them.

WATCH IT IF IN THE MOOD FOR SOMETHING:
Charming, Humane, Thought-provoking, Well-acted

RATING:
MPAA R

LANGUAGE:
Spanish

STARRING:
Daniel Giménez Cacho, Gael García Bernal, Maribel Verdú

WRITTEN BY:
Alfonso Cuarón, Carlos Cuarón

DIRECTED BY:
Alfonso Cuarón

ROMANCE | **THE SUGGESTIONS** | 92

Strictly Ballroom 1992

★★★★★

Strictly Ballroom is an energetic, fun and hilarious movie. Baz Lurhman does an incredible job telling the story of a rebellious young dancer who just wants to dance his own steps in the face of conformity. When he finds an inexperienced yet determined dance partner it's the beginning of an unexpected love story like no other. This movie isn't like the usual rom-com, it has colour, vitality and passion. It's a Moulin Rouge but with even more character, and the work that put Lurhman on the map for everyone.

WATCH IT IF IN THE MOOD FOR SOMETHING:
Well-acted

RATING:
PG

LANGUAGE:
English

STARRING:
Bill Hunter, Paul Mercurio, Tara Morice

WRITTEN BY:
Baz Luhrmann

DIRECTED BY:
Baz Lurhman

ROMANCE | **THE SUGGESTIONS** | 93

Adventureland 2009

★★★★☆

Adventureland is a retro-tinged movie about teens in Pittsburgh working at a run down amusement park during the summer of 1987. It is marketed as similar to Superbad, when in fact the only thing they have in common is the Director. Adventureland is funny, but it is more sweet, tender, and intimate.

Touching on themes of unrequited love, returning home, and small-town love, the film stars Jesse Eisenberg, Kristen Stewart, and the always-delightful-duo of Bill Hader and Kristen Wiig. In addition, the film's soundtrack is a joyous blast from the past, running the gamut of all your favorite 1980's synth-happy love songs. It is a movie that anyone can really relate to, no matter when they were born, and an amazing watch.

WATCH IT IF IN THE MOOD FOR SOMETHING:
Beautiful, Charming, Romantic, Simple, Sweet, Uplifting

RATING:
R

LANGUAGE:
English

STARRING:
Jesse Eisenberg, Kristen Stewart, Ryan Reynolds

WRITTEN BY:
Greg Mottola

DIRECTED BY:
Greg Mottola

Sci-Fi & Fantasy

SCI-FI | **THE SUGGESTIONS** | 94

Moon 2009

★★★★★

Moon is a sci-fi movie that doesn't care that it's a sci-fi movie. It's not about space exploration or aliens. It's about a man struggling to understand what and who he is and the dehumanizing effect of industrialization. Moon leaves you with a pit in your stomach and an incredible feeling of melancholy. It is perfectly acted by Sam Rockwell and the voice of Kevin Spacey. Moon keeps you guessing and deeply enthralled. A true masterpiece I would recommend to anyone, whether they are sci-fi nerds or just movie lovers.

WATCH IT IF IN THE MOOD FOR SOMETHING:
Thought-provoking

RATING:
R

LANGUAGE:
English

STARRING:
Dominique McElligott, Kevin Spacey, Sam Rockwell

WRITTEN BY:
Duncan Jones, Nathan Parker

DIRECTED BY:
Duncan Jones

SCI-FI | **THE SUGGESTIONS** | 95

Mr. Nobody 2009

★★★★☆

Based on a beautiful premise, sprinkled with artistic vision, it is an intelligent sit back and relax movie. The film explores the life and times of Nemo Nobody, the last mortal man on earth, as he reflects on the important choices he's made. Each of these choices are presented as branching pathways of what could have been, utilizing innovative non-linear cinematography. In addition to the film's winning structure, its soundtrack is considered a masterpiece, perfectly fitting the plot via looping and trilling melodies. The film garnered 6 Margaritte awards, and has slowly been developing into an indie cult classic.

WATCH IT IF IN THE MOOD FOR SOMETHING:
Challenging, Gripping, Mysterious, Thought-provoking, Weird

RATING:
R

LANGUAGE:
English

STARRING:
Diane Kruger, Jared Leto, Sarah Polley

WRITTEN BY:
Jaco Van Dormael

DIRECTED BY:
Jaco Van Dormael

SCI-FI | **THE SUGGESTIONS** | 96

The Road 2009

★★★☆☆

A Cormac McCarthy novel adaptation (like No Country for Old Men), The Road is an apocalypse movie set in a 'scorched Earth' rendition of the world. It follows a father (played by Viggo Mortensen) and his son as they battle to survive everyday life. Throughout the movie, the son's trust in his father grows and shrinks depending on choices the father makes, as he attempts to protect his son from cannibals, bandits, and the threat of starvation. The gritty realism this movie presents sets it apart from many other more theatrical releases, with the setting of a charred world illustrating a rather depressing new reality. A very down to earth and heartfelt story. Definitely worth the watch if you're willing to feel like you've been punched in the gut.

WATCH IT IF IN THE MOOD FOR SOMETHING:
Gripping, Raw

RATING:
R

LANGUAGE:
English

STARRING:
Charlize Theron,
Kodi Smit-McPhee,
Viggo Mortensen

WRITTEN BY:
Cormac McCarthy,
Joe Penhall

DIRECTED BY:
John Hillcoat

shows

SHOWS | THE ORIGINALS | 97

Abstract: The Art of Design 2017

GENRE:
Documentary

★★★★★

Each episode of Abstract is a look into an art discipline through the lens of a selected contemporary pioneer. From illustration to footwear design, the show follows how the artists create and live, how they got started, etc. The documentary itself is really aesthetically pleasing, which kind of taps into your own creativity. The designers in the series are unknowingly well-known. Does that make sense? You will instantly recognize their work even though you've never heard of them before. A light, easy-going and inspirational documentary.

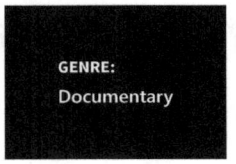

RATING:
TV-14

STARRING:
Elisabeth Biondi, Ilse Crawford, Platon

DURATION:
30 minutes to 1 hour

CREATED BY:
Scott Dadich

SHOWS | THE ORIGINALS | 98

American Vandal 2017

★★★☆☆

With so many popular true crime programs like Making a Murderer, The Keepers and The Jinx, you must have seen something like this coming – a satirical true crime series. Although that sounds like a silly idea to go over in many episodes, trust me, this show is amazing. I don't know if it's the genius of its makers or just the magic of this golden TV show era we live in, but what starts as a joke actually ends up being a pretty compelling mystery. 27 teachers of a high school find their cars vandalized – with drawings of penises. The suspected senior, Dylan Maxwell (already known for drawing penises everywhere) is then expelled. A sophomore student then takes it upon himself to investigate and prove Dylan's innocence. Hilarious, yes, but this show is actually also very captivating.

GENRE:
Comedy, Mystery

RATING:
MPAA TV-MA

STARRING:
Griffin Gluck, Jimmy Tatro, Tyler Alvarez

DURATION:
Under 30 Minutes

CREATED BY:
Dan Perrault, Tony Yacenda

SHOWS | THE ORIGINALS | 99

Atypical 2017

★★☆☆☆

Keir Gilchrist who you may know from the movie It's Kind of a Funny Story plays Sam, an 18-year-old on the autistic spectrum trying to navigate the "typical" aspects of a teenager's life: dating, independence, friendships, etc. Perhaps people dealing with autism can better attest to this, but the show feels genuine and realistic. Don't get me wrong, it's a comedy, but it's a really heartfelt approach to the funny sitcom format. In a lot of ways, Atypical is the perfect 2017 Netflix-age coming-of-age sitcom: it's funny and smart, but also keen to be realistic. And Atypical is about Sam's family almost as much as it is about him, and how they adjust to his new quest for self-discovery. Look out for newcomer Brigette Lundy-Paine, who does an amazing job playing Sam's siter Casey!

GENRE:
Comedy, Drama

RATING:
TV-MA

STARRING:
Amy Okuda, Brigette Lundy-Paine, Jennifer Jason Leigh, Keir Gilchrist

DURATION:
Under 30 Minutes

CREATED BY:
Robia Rashid

SHOWS | THE ORIGINALS | 100

Bloodline 2015, 2016, 2017

★★★☆☆

Named as a successor to Breaking Bad in its approach to storytelling, Bloodline is a superb series about a contemporary American family and the secrets it hides. After the black sheep son, Danny, returns to the family, he threatens to expose these secrets. The family is torn between protecting themselves and trying to take him back.

Bloodline is undeniably slow-burning, so it might take a bit of patience at first, but once you get used to the rhythm, and find yourself more comfortable with the Florida Keys, the payoff is hot fire. It waits for you to be comfortable to make you uncomfortable, so to speak. It manages to be very authentic, and puts off series clichés to come up with a believable storyline.

GENRE:
Drama, Mystery

RATING:
MPAA
TV-MA

STARRING:
Ben Mendelsohn, Kyle Chandler, Linda Cardellini

DURATION:
30 minutes to 1 hour

CREATED BY:
Daniel Zelman, Glenn Kessler, Todd A. Kessler

SHOWS | THE ORIGINALS | 101

Chef's Table 2015, 2016

★★★★★

A look into the interesting lives and magnificent plates made in the kitchens of some of the best chefs in the world (including an episode with the best). Each episode dives deep into their worlds', providing an intimate and ultimately inspiring look at their life both inside the kitchen and out; with all of them having lived unique lives to say the least. Their perspectives on everything from family life to entrepreneurship will dazzle you almost as much as the colorful and spectacular dishes they produce.

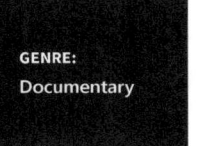

GENRE:
Documentary

RATING:
MPAA
TV-MA

STARRING:
Bill Buford, Dan Barber, Massimo Bottura

DURATION:
30 minutes to 1 hour

SHOWS | THE ORIGINALS | 102

Collateral 2018

★★★☆☆

This BBC/Netflix show stars Carey Mulligan (Drive, Pride & Prejudice, An Education) as DI Kip, a detective investigating a seemingly random killing of a pizza delivery man. Her acting, added to other amazing performances, make what would otherwise be slow and careful writing truly lively. It's four episodes only (one for each day), and leaves no questions unanswered. A breeze of a show, it's rich in back stories that will keep you intrigued until the very end.

GENRE:
Mystery

RATING:
TV-MA

STARRING:
Carey Mulligan, Jeany Spark, Nicola Walker

DURATION:
30 minutes to 1 hour

SHOWS | THE ORIGINALS | 103

Dark 2017

★★★★★

If you liked Stranger Things but are sick of the hype, sit tight because there is a lot more of where that came from in Dark.

Here is what they have in common: the aesthetic, great music, and they're both about the disappearance of a child. Other than that, it is very difficult to compare Dark to anything else we've seen before.

The show is compelling and complex which makes it incredibly tension ridden. Each episode will draw you deeper into the plot until you become completely obsessed with finding out what is going to happen.

This German town has a long and heavy history, which is brought to the forefront of the collective conscious when a child goes missing. The plot twists and turns through decades of history – and that's as much as we will share without ruining it for you.

This is without a doubt Netflix's most twisted show to date! It is also Netflix's first German show – we recommend watching the subtitled version so you don't miss getting the full range of emotions from the actors.

GENRE:
Mystery

RATING:
MPAA
Not Rated

STARRING:
Jördis Triebel,
Karoline Eichhorn,
Oliver Masucci

DURATION:
30 minutes to 1 hour

CREATED BY:
Baran bo Odar,
Jantje Friese

SHOWS | THE ORIGINALS | 104

Dix pour cent 2015, 2017

★★★★☆

Think of Dix pour cent, or as it was horribly translated to English "Call My Agent!", as a smart French version of the American show Entourage. It's the kind of thing where if you like it you will become obsessed with it. It chronicles the life of an aspiring agent at a French casting agency. New to Paris, she lands a job and is confronted with a variety of very stressed characters. Dix pour cent is the perfect definition of a hidden gem, featuring countless guest appearances by famous French actors and actresses.

GENRE:
Comedy

RATING:
Not Rated

STARRING:
Camille Cottin, Grégory Montel, Thibault de Montalembert

DURATION:
30 minutes to 1 hour

CREATED BY:
Fanny Herrero

SHOWS | THE ORIGINALS | 105

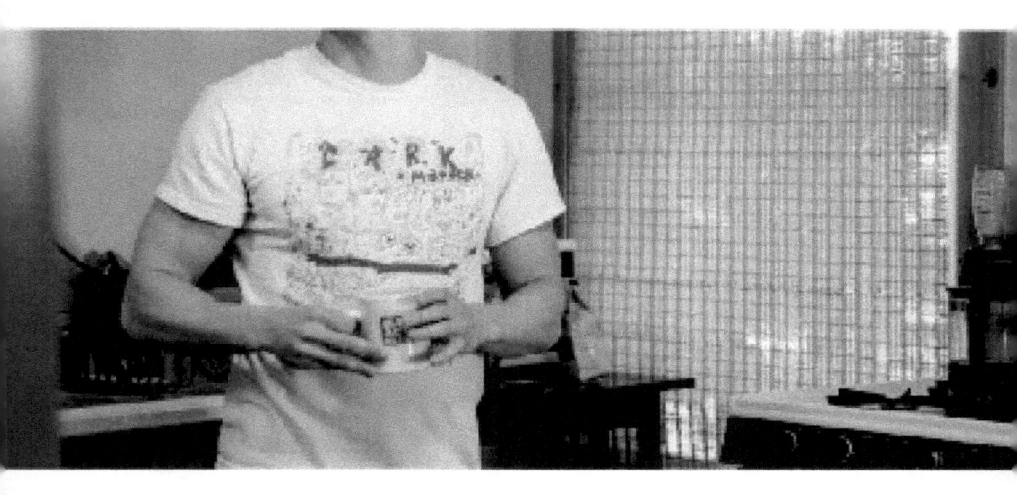

Easy 2016

★★★☆☆

There may not be a show or movie out there that the term "slice-of-life" applies to better than Easy. Don't watch it expecting stuff to happen, it won't. I mean it will, but don't expect any big plot twists, and don't anticipate the end of episodes: enjoy it as it happens.

With different stories in each 30-minute episode, Joe Swanberg (Drinking Buddies) who created, wrote and directed will feel as the only constant throughout the series. Yet, as you move through it, you realize that other than being mini-cameos to each other, these characters share many of the same defining elements of modern-day culture. The ways they navigate relationships, sex, and technology is relevant and realistic.

GENRE:
Comedy

RATING:
TV-MA

STARRING:
Jane Adams, Marc Maron, Michael Chernus, Zazie Beetz

DURATION:
Under 30 Minutes

CREATED BY:
Joe Swanberg

SHOWS | THE ORIGINALS | 106

Flint Town 2018

★★★★★

A captivating documentary series on the struggling state of the police department in Flint, Michigan; and by extension a large proportion of American cities. The town that had made the news for its water crisis is home to another crisis that dates back further: an exponential rise in crime. The police department, however, keeps losing funding year over year, so much so that they can only have less than 9 one-officer cars patrolling the (large) city at any one time. A sobering and impressive account that follows officers facing not only harrowing situations in a failing city, but also the constant fear of being laid-off.

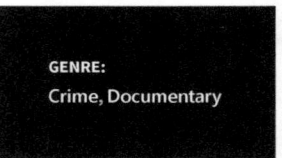

GENRE:
Crime, Documentary

RATING:
TV-MA

STARRING:
James Tolbert,
Karen Weaver,
Wayne Suttles

DURATION:
Under 30 Minutes

CREATED BY:
Drea Cooper,
Jessica Dimmock,
Zackary Canepari

SHOWS | THE ORIGINALS | 107

GLOW 2017

★★★★★

In an age where every show gets called "original" the minute after it comes out, this amazing series from the creators of Orange is the New Black will actually make you go "no, that show is different!". Starring an almost all-women cast (except for the coach, played masterfully by podcast icon Marc Maron), it's the story of how a crazy wrestling show was put together in the 1980s called Gorgeous Ladies of Wrestling. Alison Brie (Community) plays the girl at the center of the effort to make this show happen, having had a terribly failed career thus far. Perfectly acted and featuring funny as well as absurd moments, GLOW is a great show that you can binge on Netflix without noticing the episodes fly by.

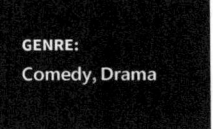

GENRE:
Comedy, Drama

RATING:
TV-MA

STARRING:
Alison Brie, Betty Gilpin, Britney Young, Marc Maron, Sydelle Noel

DURATION:
Under 30 Minutes

CREATED BY:
Carly Mensch, Liz Flahive

SHOWS | THE ORIGINALS | 108

Godless 2017

★★★★☆

Violent, very Western, and in a breath of fresh air: female. Godless is a show about strong bad-ass women that govern their own town in the late 1800s. Roy Goode is their visitor, an outlaw chased by another, much worse outlaw, Frank Griffin. It's an honest and powerful show with some amazing performances, and even more amazing aesthetics. If you love Westerns but find them too predictable, this show was made for you.

GENRE:
Drama

RATING:
MPAA
TV-MA

STARRING:
Jack O'Connell, Michelle Dockery, Scoot McNairy

DURATION:
30 minutes to 1 hour

CREATED BY:
Scott Frank

SHOWS | THE ORIGINALS | 109

Love 2016, 2017

★★★☆☆

About love as much as it is about loneliness, romance as much as realism and the longing for a genuine connection as much as being tired of that longing – this is a smart and well nuanced series on building relationships. It follows Gus and Mickey, two damaged people trying to recover from bad breakups. They're respectively played by writer/creater Paul Rust and Gillian Jacobs (Britta from Community). Love portrays their love story as an example of relationships by default, chemistry that stems more from the need to be in a relationship than any physical or intellectual attraction. And it features many hilarious sequences, some are cleverly composed jokes but most of them are the painfully-real type.

GENRE:
Comedy

RATING:
TV-MA

STARRING:
Claudia O'Doherty, Gillian Jacobs, Paul Rust

DURATION:
Under 30 Minutes

CREATED BY:
Judd Apatow, Lesley Arfin

SHOWS | THE ORIGINALS | 110

Lovesick 2014, 2016, 2018

★★★★★

A British comedy series that was originally called Scrotal Recall before it was bought by Netflix and rebranded. It's about Dylan and his friends, he is a desperate romantic in his 20s who suddenly discovers he has chlamydia, and therefore must contact all his (numerous) past sexual adventures and relationships.
Every episode has the name of one of the girls he has to contact, and the story that goes with it. Dylan's best friends are Luke, a hilarious seemingly confident but actually insecure, shallow business-school-type; and Eve, Dylan's best friend who may have undisclosed feelings for him, she is a sarcastic, smart girl who is very well portrayed by Misfits star Antonia Thomas.
Lovesick is a charming little series, that portrays failed relationships but ends up being beautifully romantic. Something you can easily find yourself watching many episodes in one take.

GENRE:
Comedy, Romance

RATING:
TV-MA

STARRING:
Antonia Thomas, Daniel Ings, Johnny Flynn

DURATION:
Under 30 Minutes

CREATED BY:
Tom Edge

SHOWS | THE ORIGINALS | 111

Manhunt: Unabomber

2017

★★★★★

A dramatic take on the life and capture of Ted Kaczynski, popularly known as UNABOMBER(UNiversity and Airline BOMber) from the eyes of an FBI profiler. Kaczynski was responsible for 16 bombings, and it took 17 years for the FBI to catch him. To date, he's the target of the most expensive chase the FBI has ever launched. The show is not a mystery (facts are the matter of public domain) and doesn't even pretend to be one. Instead, it focuses on the complex motives of the UNABOMBER, as well as the bureaucracy that the FBI ran through trying to catch him. It's a really well-made, engrossing show that's hard not to watch in one take. It's 8 episodes of 40 minutes, so pick the time you start it wisely.

GENRE:
Crime, Mystery

RATING:
TV-14

STARRING:
Ben Weber, Jeremy Bobb, Sam Worthington

DURATION:
30 minutes to 1 hour

CREATED BY:
Andrew Sodroski, Jim Clemente, Tony Gittelson

SHOWS | THE ORIGINALS | 112

Marco Polo 2014, 2016

★★★★☆

This colossal-budget show ($90 million for the first season alone) never caught a break. Somehow it didn't make it to the big audience it deserved. It tells the grand story of Marco Polo the explorer, and the years he spent with the Mongols, going back forth in their ranks between prisoner and leader. It was during this crucial time for the empire that Kublai Khan had extended the reach of his empire even further than his more famous grandfather Genghis Khan. As you'd expect with a show featuring this many characters and such a new world, the first season is not as entertaining as could be, but the show becomes its full-self as a true epic in season 2.

GENRE:
Drama

RATING:
TV-MA

STARRING:
Benedict Wong, Joan Chen, Lorenzo Richelmy

DURATION:
30 minutes to 1 hour

CREATED BY:
John Fusco

SHOWS | THE ORIGINALS | 113

Master of None 2015, 2017

★★★★☆

Master of None doesn't take a shot at realism that it doesn't nail. It doesn't take that many, since its main goal, and something both the show and its creator Aziz Ansari do very well, can be summarized in one word: charm. Quirky everything: acting, story line, soundtracks. And because it is the age of augmented realism in TV, this show feels fresh and timely. It features the life of Dev, a smart and funny actor as he tackles professional success, a serious relationship and growing up. Dev the character is based on the creator of the show and its lead actor Aziz Ansari. Because of this but also because of the genuineness of its creators and the wonderful casting, everything here is done with heart. Last thing, Master of None has got to be the most binge-worthy sitcom! You might want to think twice before starting it. You've been warned.

GENRE:
Comedy

RATING:
MPAA TV-MA

STARRING:
Aziz Ansari, Eric Wareheim, Lena Waithe

DURATION:
Under 30 Minutes

CREATED BY:
Alan Yang, Aziz Ansari

SHOWS | THE ORIGINALS | 114

Mindhunter 2017

★★★★★

An exquisite crime show made under the supervision of David Fincher. It's a beautifully retro account of the start of serial murders and law enforcement's early attempts to understand them. When his role as a negotiator comes to an abrupt end, agent Holden Ford becomes involved with the freshly founded Behavioral Science Unit headed by agent Bill Tench (marvelously played by Holt McCallany). Together they go around the country interviewing serial killers and trying to solve open murder cases. Possibly Netflix's most binge-worthy show so far, Mindhunter is a very interesting, almost scientifically oriented thriller.

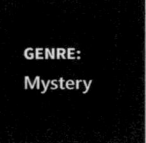

GENRE:
Mystery

RATING:
MPAA | TV-MA

STARRING:
Anna Torv, Holt McCallany, Jonathan Groff

DURATION:
30 minutes to 1 hour

CREATED BY:
Joe Penhall

SHOWS | THE ORIGINALS | 115

Money Heist 2017

★★★★★

Smart, suspensful, original, and just all-around a perfect show. Money Heist (La casa de papel) is 13 episodes about a gang who embarks on the biggest heist in history – not just in their country of Spain but everywhere. Led by an enigmatic character only known as The Professor, the rest of the gang adopts city names: Tokyo, Rio, Helsinki, Nairobi, etc. Their roles in the heist are as different as their personalities and approach to relationships. The script is insanely suspenseful, super fast when it needs to, and painfully slow when you don't want it to be (and when it's perfect for it to be), taking you into the heist that quickly becomes a chess game between The Professor and the police. Be ready to get instantly hooked into a very binge-worthy journey.
A truly amazing show, and one of the best if not the best heist TV show ever made.

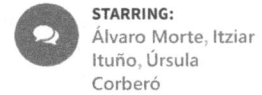

GENRE:
Action, Mystery

RATING:
MPAA
TV-MA

STARRING:
Álvaro Morte, Itziar Ituño, Úrsula Corberó

DURATION:
30 minutes to 1 hour

CREATED BY:
Álex Pina

SHOWS | THE ORIGINALS | 116

Mushishi 2005

★★★★☆

Mushishi is one of those shows that you watch one episode at a time to relax after a long day of work. It's a slow, atmospheric animation about a world where peculiar plant-like creatures called Mushi live alongside humans who are usually unaware of them. Think of Mushi as the most basic form of life. While being purposeless, they can unintentionally have a wide variety of effects on humans, sometimes helping them but always at an unforeseen cost. Ginko is a traveler who studies Mushi and on his way helps villagers with their problems.Each episode is an independent short story about a chapter of Ginko's travels. The stories feel weirdly the same as folklore you grew up with. They are comfy, they hold a few moral lessons at the end of each one, and they're sometimes scary and thought-provoking. Despite being "anime", this show might as well be a genre on its own. It holds none of the stereotypes surrounding anime, and it's really just a collection of solid short stories coupled with great animation and an amazing soundtrack. If you're tired and need a show to watch late at night with a loved one or by yourself, pick an episode at random and see for yourself how great of a show this is.

GENRE:
Animation

RATING:
Not Rated

STARRING:
Kôjun Itô, Travis Willingham, Yûto Nakano

DURATION:
Under 30 Minutes

CREATED BY:
Hiroshi Nagahama

SHOWS | THE ORIGINALS | 117

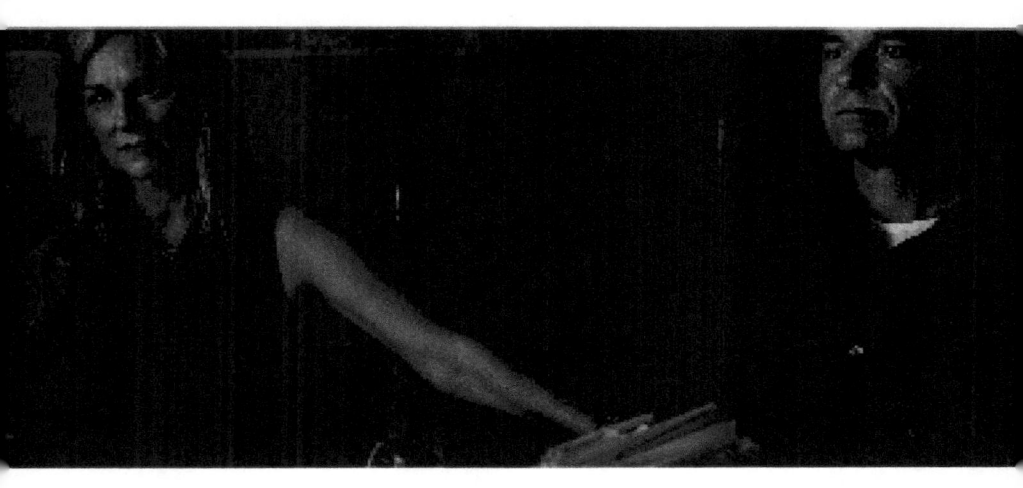

Ozark 2017

★★★★☆

Ozark is a show about how a seemingly average family that gets tangled up in very unusual circumstances. Jason Bateman plays an accountant who launders money for a big Mexican drug cartel from Chicago. When things go wrong with the Cartel leader, he is forced to set up shop in the Ozark valley and change practically every aspect of his wife and two kids' lives. The show is not only an exciting crime drama but an interesting manifestation of very common American family discussions and concerns.

GENRE:
Crime, Drama

RATING:
TV-MA

STARRING:
Jason Bateman, Laura Linney, Sofia Hublitz

DURATION:
30 minutes to 1 hour

CREATED BY:
Bill Dubuque, Mark Williams

SHOWS | THE ORIGINALS | 118

Terrace House 2015

★★★☆☆

Terrace House is the perfect show to binge on a lazy day, it will make you feel intimate not only with its cast, but also with the Japanese culture and lifestyle. The premise here is nothing that hasn't been done before, and usually very terribly: Six strangers -three boys and three girls in their twenties – are given a beautiful home to live in for several months in Tokyo. We get to observe their interactions and the slow building of their friendships. What sets it apart from others in its genre is that it's wholly unscripted and nothing is forced. The cast are normal people whose lives don't revolve around the show: they have jobs, they're free to come and leave the house whenever they want, they can travel, sleep all day, or date people not on the show. You might think this makes for bad TV, but it really doesn't: Terrace House is really well-made and it knows how to make mundane life interesting and engaging. To round it up another cast of established japanese entertainers appear on interludes each episode to share their opinions on the happenings inside the house and to offer some comedic insight.

GENRE:
Drama, Romance

RATING:
Not Rated

STARRING:
Azusa Babazono, Reina Triendl, Yoshimi Tokui

DURATION:
Under 30 Minutes

CREATED BY:
Fuji Television, Netflix

SHOWS | THE ORIGINALS | 119

The End of the F***cking World 2018

GENRE: Mystery, Romance

★★★★★

An amazing binge-worthy show that is a mix between a coming-of-age story, a romance, and a crime thriller.

It tells the story of James, a 17-year-old who believes he is a psychopath (for some very convincing reasons). James decides he wants the victim of his first murder to be a new schoolmate, Alyssa. He befriends her and keeps waiting for the perfect moment to kill Alyssa until he finds himself on a journey with her to escape her home.

Somewhere near the middle of the show, and without you fully realizing it, it transforms from an original coming-of-age story or odd-boy-meets-odd-girl story to an intriguing view on adolescent insecurities and the role of parents into shaping them. It transforms from a mysterious, almost charming story to an interesting character study. This is when the show will blow your mind. It's a fresh, smart, funny yet disturbing emotional thrill ride.

RATING: MPAA TV-MA

STARRING: Alex Lawther, Jessica Barden, Steve Oram

DURATION: Under 30 Minutes

SHOWS | THE ORIGINALS | 120

The Get Down 2016, 2017

★★★★☆

Watch out for Ezekiel in this show, he will steal your heart. And also please sit through the first episode. Yes, it's long, but if you get The Get Down, it is one of the best shows on Netflix. Created by Baz Luhrmann and Pulitzer Prize winning playwright Stephen Adly Guirgis, it narrates the rise of hip-hop in a broken 1970's New York. The impressive credentials don't stop there, as the series is narrated by Nas, features work by four-time Academy Award winner Catherine Martin as well as hip-hop historian Nelson George. It is perhaps for this reason that the word "narration" takes its full meaning here. Every episode, every scene, every character are made with extreme care, resulting in sometimes longer than necessary sequences. A sacrifice that will make some viewers very happy, but which many might have a hard time adjusting to.

GENRE:
Drama

RATING:
TV-MA

STARRING:
Herizen F. Guardiola, Justice Smith, Shameik Moore

DURATION:
Over 1 hour

CREATED BY:
Baz Luhrmann, Stephen Adly Guirgis

SHOWS | THE ORIGINALS | 121

The Good Place 2016, 2017

★★★☆☆

The Good Place is about a girl who dies and finds herself in the better side of the afterlife: The Good Place (as opposed to The Bad Place). Only problem? Someone made a mistake and she really doesn't belong there. While The Good Place is filled with people who went on humanitarian missions and saved the world – her last days were spent scamming old sick people as a drug sales rep. Starring Kristen Bell in a truly hilarious role, The Good Place is about her character's attempt to become a better person and stay away from The Bad Place. It's a very entertaining, weird, and clever show. Just watch the first episode and you will be hooked forever.

GENRE:
Comedy

RATING:
TV-PG

STARRING:
Jameela Jamil, Kristen Bell, William Jackson Harper

DURATION:
30 minutes to 1 hour

CREATED BY:
Michael Schur

SHOWS | THE ORIGINALS | 122

The Keepers 2017

★★★★☆

This is an amazing mini-series of 7 episodes marketed as being the same as the Netflix hit show Making a Murderer. While the two share some of the defining tones, The Keepers is a much more interesting show. It trades cliffhangers for substance, without compromising at all on the mystery of the murder addressed. It gives the bigger picture on what was going on in Baltimore at the time of the murder, and then heavily focuses on the victims from after the murder. It's a riveting tale of injustice, sexual abuse, and corruption. If you so much as like true crime shows (or movies like Spotlight), you're going to not only love The Keepers, but you will find it inspiring in how it addresses the uncovering of secrets.

GENRE:
Documentary, Mystery

RATING:
TV-MA

STARRING:
Abbie Schaub, Gemma Hoskins, Tom Nugent

DURATION:
30 minutes to 1 hour

CREATED BY:
Ryan White

SHOWS | THE ORIGINALS | 123

Wild Wild Country 2018

★★★★★

A Netflix documentary mini-series that follows the relocation of a cult from India to a small town in Oregon and the ensuing events. It's a completely true story, but the events it portrays are so bizarre and unexpected that they have to be seen to be believed. The cult, led by a controversial Indian guru, drew worldwide attention to its beginnings in India and then to its conflict with the locals once it relocated to the United States. If you were a contemporary, you must know that the town is Antelope and the guru is Bhagwan or Osho, but if you were not, it is very unlikely you've even heard of it. What was a very significant moment in American media and history has been long forgotten, and is retold here in a captivating way. An extremely well-executed and a powerful account of a very unlikely story.

GENRE:
Documentary

RATING:
Not Rated

STARRING:
Ma Anand Sheela, Osho, Philip Toelkes

DURATION:
30 minutes to 1 hour

SHOWS | THE SUGGESTIONS | 124

Chewing Gum 2015, 2017

★★★☆☆

A hilarious British sitcom about 24-year-old Tracey Gorden, a shop assistant living in a London housing estate with crazy friends and an even crazier family. Having had a very religious upbringing, the show is about her navigating adulthood and trying to untangle herself from the unexciting life her neighborhood offers (mainly by trying to lose her virginity). Michaela Coel plays Tracey, who also wrote and created the show. Her expressive face and fantastic character building make for such an original show. This is possibly the best sitcom on Netflix right now.

GENRE:
Comedy

RATING:
MPAA
Not Rated

STARRING:
Danielle Walters,
Michaela Coel,
Robert Lonsdale

DURATION:
Under 30 Minutes

CREATED BY:
Michaela Coel

SHOWS | THE SUGGESTIONS | 125

Luther 2010, 2011, 2013, 2015

★★★★★

An 11-time Primetime Emmy nominated BBC series. Two words: Idris Elba. This is his show. He stars as DCI John Luther (watch this show and you'll never be able to pronounce that without a British accent), an extremely smart, committed yet unpredictable and sometimes violent detective.
The creator and writer, Neil Cross (Doctor Who), has said to be inspired by a mix of Sherlock Holmes and Columbo. The show really succeeds at hitting that right balance. The only difference is that both the crimes portrayed and the context of the show are very modern.
Luther will sometimes play with your mind, entertain you at others, but mostly it will keep you captivated. And without realizing it, it will make you develop an interesting closeness with Elba's character. The supporting cast, from other police officers to villains, are all terrifically acted. This is British mystery at its very best.

GENRE:
Drama, Mystery

RATING:
MPAA TV-MA

STARRING:
Dermot Crowley, Idris Elba, Warren Brown

DURATION:
30 minutes to 1 hour

CREATED BY:
Neil Cross

SHOWS | THE SUGGESTIONS | 126

Maron 2013, 2014, 2015, 2016

★★★★☆

Big-time podcast icon and comedian Marc Maron stars as a fictionalized version of himself in this hilarious and sometimes troubling show. Maron the character is a recovering alcoholic who abuses coffee in the constant state of chase after a buzz, he is divorced, bitter, yet weirdly kind – he is always trying to be a better version of himself and failing.
The series is about his attempt at human relationships, both romantic and not, after a bad history that spans from a negligent self-centered mother to bad eating habits and self-shame. Maron is insightful, very funny, and especially in the first season, a joy to watch.

GENRE:
Comedy

RATING:
MPAA Not Rated

DURATION:
Under 30 Minutes

SHOWS | THE SUGGESTIONS | 127

The Honourable Woman 2014

★★★★☆

Think of The Honourable Woman as Homeland on steroids. In Homeland, the question was whether the main character was good or bad, in The Honourable Woman, the question is whether *anybody* is good or bad. The characters are all so well-crafted that it's difficult to ever feel comfortable with any one of them. This Netflix/BBC mini-series is set around Nessa Stein (Maggie Gyllenhaal), a heiress to a large arms company involved in the Israeli/Palestinian conflict. When her father is assassinated, her willingness to keep the business alive by diversifying it away from the war business is met with strong economic and political opposition. Easily one of the best political thrillers ever made. Won Gyllenhaal the Golden Globe for Best Actress.

GENRE:
Drama, Mystery

RATING:
Not Rated

STARRING:
Lubna Azabal,
Maggie Gyllenhaal,
Stephen Rea

DURATION:
30 minutes to 1 hour

CREATED BY:
Hugo Blick

SHOWS | THE SUGGESTIONS | 128

Top Boy 2011, 2013

★★★☆☆

The first season has four episodes, expect to watch them in one take. Top Boy is a compelling and gritty crime drama set in London about a kid who grows up in a crime filled neighborhood. His mom is admitted to hospital and he has to take care of himself in a time where two drug dealers are trying to rise and gain more control of the neighborhood. Top Boy has an intricate plot that builds a lot of tension and which will have you completely hooked, but it also has a lot of amazing non-plot related moments. It depicts the concept of morality in a neighborhood like the one portrayed, and the tough decisions its people have to make every day. If you liked The Wire, this show is for you.

GENRE:
Drama, Mystery

RATING:
Not Rated

STARRING:
Ashley Walters, Kane Robinson, Shone Romulus

DURATION:
30 minutes to 1 hour

CREATED BY:
Ronan Bennett

SHOWS | THE SUGGESTIONS | 129

Wentworth

2013, 2014, 2015, 2016, 2017

★★★★☆

Dark and almost too realistic, Wentworth is the women's prison drama that we've all been waiting for. This Australian show might have the same set-up as Orange is the New Black, following a recently incarcerated woman as she discovers a new world, but the two series couldn't be more far apart. Wentworth is more Breaking Bad than Orange is the New Black. It doesn't follow people who are wronged by the system or who are misunderstood, but women that have actually done violent things, and continue being violent in prison. Everyone appeals to their dark side, and it's almost impossible for any character to be redeemed in the viewer's eye. The show's biggest selling point though is that it never goes the violence-for-violence route, its immaculate character development allows to find reason and authenticity behind every act. This a true hidden gem.

GENRE:
Drama

RATING:
TV-MA

STARRING:
Celia Ireland, Kate Atkinson, Leanne Campbell

DURATION:
30 minutes to 1 hour

CREATED BY:
Lara Radulovich, Reg Watson

A big thank you to our contributors:
Bilal Zouheir, Tara Goe, Graham, Richard, Jamie Rutherford, Christina Hale, Tyler, Christina Ienna, Ignacio Guibert, Low, Melanie, Juan Manuel, Ashley Mantha-Hollands, Anass, Laura, Connor, Thu Phuong T, Vojta, Josh Billings, Hugo Bernard, Morgan, Anass Boudiga, Pablo, Bill Beavis, H D Williams, Laurine, Michelle, Akshay Naik, Sam Cheng, Jonfen, Ankit Aggarwal, Katy, Sienna Orlando-Lalaguna, Valentine Dessertenne, Utathya Ghosh, Lewis Everett.

Edited by the lovely Ashley Mantha-Hollands.

CPSIA information can be obtained
at www.ICGtesting.com
Printed in the USA
BVHW050605030123
655447BV00018B/243

9 781986 862509